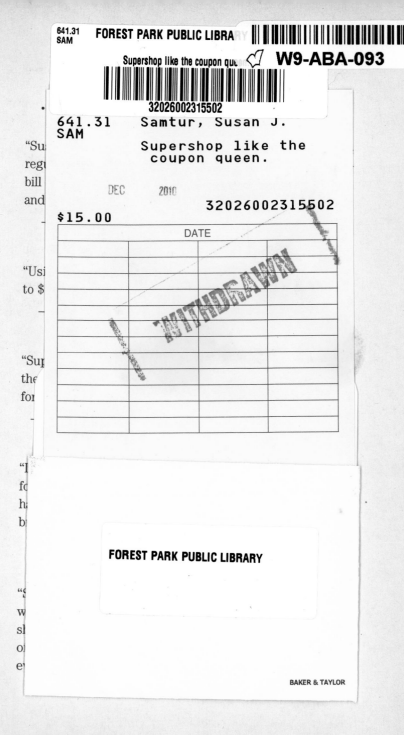

"Susan Samtur rocks the grocery store. You will have to see her bill to believe: $181 for $18 bucks."

—**Victoria Spilabotte**, KNBC-TV (Los Angeles, CA)

❖

"Smart shoppers [who follow Samtur's advice] are still making a killing when they go to the supermarket."

—**John McCaa**, WABC WFFA-TV (Dallas, TX)

❖

"There may be no such thing as a free lunch, but Susan Samtur has come pretty close. She's the nation's undisputed 'Coupon Queen.' And, all its takes is a trip to the grocery store with her to understand why. Everything Susan buys she gets for pennies on the dollar."

—**Nancy Pender**, FOX (Chicago, IL)

❖

"[Samtur gives us] all the more reason . . . to be clipping coupons. I have a new incentive, I'm committed."

—**Courtney Gilmore**, NBC HPRC (Houston, TX)

❖

"But can [Samtur] really get this cart full of groceries for less than $20? We'll see. I can't believe what I just saw . . . I'm in shock!"

—**Nydia Han**, NBC WPVI (Philadelphia, PA)

SUPERSHOP LIKE THE COUPON QUEEN

*How to Save 50% or More
Every Time You Shop*

SUSAN SAMTUR

with ADAM R. SAMTUR

B

BERKLEY BOOKS, NEW YORK

THE BERKLEY PUBLISHING GROUP
Published by the Penguin Group
Penguin Group (USA) Inc.
375 Hudson Street, New York, New York 10014, USA

Penguin Group (Canada), 90 Eglinton Avenue East, Suite 700, Toronto, Ontario M4P 2Y3, Canada
(a division of Pearson Penguin Canada Inc.)
Penguin Books Ltd., 80 Strand, London WC2R 0RL, England
Penguin Group Ireland, 25 St. Stephen's Green, Dublin 2, Ireland (a division of Penguin Books Ltd.)
Penguin Group (Australia), 250 Camberwell Road, Camberwell, Victoria 3124, Australia
(a division of Pearson Australia Group Pty. Ltd.)
Penguin Books India Pvt. Ltd., 11 Community Centre, Panchsheel Park, New Delhi—110 017, India
Penguin Group (NZ), 67 Apollo Drive, Rosedale, North Shore, 0632, New Zealand
(a division of Pearson New Zealand Ltd.)
Penguin Books (South Africa) (Pty.) Ltd., 24 Sturdee Avenue, Rosebank, Johannesburg 2196,
South Africa

Penguin Books Ltd., Registered Offices: 80 Strand, London WC2R 0RL, England

The publisher does not have any control over and does not assume any responsibility for author
or third-party websites or their content.

PRINTING HISTORY
Berkley trade paperback edition / September 2010

Library of Congress Cataloging-in-Publication Data

Samtur, Susan J.
   Supershop like the coupon queen : how to save 50% or more every time you shop / Susan J.
Samtur with Adam R. Samtur.
      p. cm.
   Includes bibliographical references and index.
   ISBN 978-0-425-23649-9 (alk. paper)
   1. Grocery shopping. 2. Consumer education. 3. Coupons (Retail trade) I. Samtur, Adam R.
   II. Title.
   TX356.S263 2010
   641.3'1—dc22
                                    2010013489

PRINTED IN THE UNITED STATES OF AMERICA

10   9   8   7   6   5   4   3   2   1

I would like to thank my children, Stuart, Mark, Michael, and Adam, who have encouraged me throughout this process.

A special note to my husband, Steve, who has always been my most ardent supporter.

I would like to dedicate this book to the memory of my father, Leon Honickman, the best Super-shopper of them all. I love you, Dad.

Contents

∙∙∙

SUPERSHOP
LIKE THE
COUPON
QUEEN

Introduction

....

The History of Supershopping

I **STARTED THE COUPONING** and refunding revolution with my 1979 bestselling book, *Cashing In at the Checkout*, and have helped millions of people save money at the supermarket.

Cashing In at the Checkout began with: "It was only about two decades ago that a bottle of Coca-Cola cost you five cents. Today, the standard size bottle will run you from thirty-five to sixty-five cents. I hate to guess what it will cost by the time my children are grown." Well, today my children are grown, and the average price of a bottle of Coke is about one dollar. Not bad after thirty years. However, things aren't so good for the majority of grocery products. The average prices of eggs, milk, and bread have risen over 420%. Unfortunately, these are items that we all need to buy on a regular basis. Manufacturers know this, which is why they are able to raise the prices. This is, after all, a supply-and-demand economy.

As I write this, the current economic climate isn't rosy. Unemployment rates are high and rising, and homes are going into foreclosure at an alarming rate. And although many experts predict that the worst is over, people are still facing rough times. We're all looking to cut costs wherever we can, and I know I can help.

In this new book, I want to introduce my brand-new, simple and comprehensive five-step Supershopping System, which can save you 50% or more at the checkout every time you shop. Yes, I said 50%. In fact, a seasoned Supershopper can save 75%, 85%, even 95% on grocery bills. But before I share my Supershopper secrets, I need to take you back to when it all started.

It was 1971: President Nixon was in office, Disney World just opened in Florida, and many Americans, including myself, were in need of extra money. I lived in a small apartment in the Bronx with my husband, Steve. We were both working as New York City schoolteachers, trying to make ends meet. I soon began collecting coupons to save money, something I had often seen my mother do. I immediately saw a reduction in my grocery bill, but I discovered that coupons alone were not enough. I started experimenting with different supermarket savings strategies. I tried everything from changing the stores I shopped at to buying in bulk, and everything in between. After about a year of this, I had finally fine-tuned my strategy and was now saving over 50% every time I went shopping.

Shortly thereafter, it dawned on me that I had to start spreading the word. So from the faculty room at my school was born *Refundle Bundle* magazine, which alerts consumers every month to over $400 in current refund and coupon offers. The magazine includes tips, Internet savings, coupon swapping, and company information packed into forty-eight pages. Creating the magazine was an enjoyable learning experience. Everything was done manually in those days. I wrote it up on a typewriter, used manual printing equipment, and printed up the magazine

> After *Cashing In at the Checkout* was published, I was considered the leading expert at saving money at the supermarket. The year before, I was given the title of "Coupon Queen" by Betty Furness of NBC's *Today*. I hold that title with great pride, having been the first "Coupon Queen" in the country, probably the world.

one copy at a time. In 1973 I began selling *Refundle Bundle* for profit. It soared in popularity, boasting over 410,000 subscribers from its original thirteen. I felt great satisfaction from helping those who needed it; something that has remained important to me to this day.

In 1976, when our first son was born, I took a leave of absence from teaching and became a more dedicated coupon shopper. I honed my skills so well that in February 1978, armed with my coupons and *Refundle Bundle*, Steve and I journeyed down to the NBC studios at Rockefeller Plaza to suggest an on-air shopping trip. The producers agreed, and a few days later a camera crew followed me around the store and watched me cut my bill from $130.18 to $7.07. The segment was so successful that I received over 150,000 letters in the mail from people eager to learn more about my system. Along with all the mail came requests from other local and national television shows to repeat this shopping feat. The response was overwhelming. We toured the nation, doing radio and newspaper interviews and television appearances on *Live with Regis and Kathie Lee*, *The Oprah Winfrey: People Are Talking Show*, *The Richard Simmons Show*, and many others.

After *Cashing In at the Checkout* was published, I was considered the leading expert at saving money at the supermarket. The year before, I was given the title of "Coupon Queen" by Betty Furness of NBC's *Today*. I hold that title with great pride, having been the first "Coupon Queen" in the country, probably the world.

Today, more than thirty years later, my children are all grown and have graduated college. They are doing very well in their careers and, like me, have learned to save in every aspect of their lives. Even after all these years, I still have the same goal of helping people to save money. Except now I have expanded my system into the digital era with the launch of three websites, a Facebook group, articles throughout the blogosphere, and a new and improved version of my Select Coupon Program, which I will discuss later. Then, of course, there is this book.

Supershop Like the Coupon Queen once again reinvents the way people shop and save at the supermarket. My unique five-step Supershopping System is the first approach that:

❖ converges new supermarket savings technologies with traditional proven techniques
❖ takes a deep look into the new technological tools that are available
❖ provides a new and accessible revision of my original Supershopping System

Every supermarket savings strategy or program that has ever been created is probably based, in some form, on mine, but I have yet to see one that can save you as much money and time as my Supershopping System. Unlike most other systems out there, Supershopping is a complete and comprehensive strategy that integrates every facet of saving into a concise, step-by-step program that requires far less time and research than other, more convoluted programs.

So it is with great pleasure that I introduce *Supershop Like the Coupon Queen*. It is my hope that you will use this book as a guide to formulate your own attack plan next time you hit the grocery store. My technique is proven; there is no reason you cannot save just as much as I do. I vowed long ago never again to pay full price for my groceries, and I want you never to pay full price either.

SUPERSHOPPING: A SYSTEM OVERVIEW

The term "Supershopper" describes a shopper armed with coupons and knowledge of store sales, one who concentrates on finding every discount and deal out there. The Supershopper compares prices, product sizes, introductory specials, and manufacturers' specially marked packages, using all of these tools to save money on bills.

Today, about 80% of all consumers use coupons, at least occasionally, to help reduce their grocery bills. But more than just using coupons, Supershopping integrates every aspect involved in lowering costs, and it is the only system out there that incorporates new technology to make your shopping experience that much more pleasurable.

Supershopping is more than a simple strategy—it is a shopping mindset. I like to think of it as buying smart, saving big. Many people see my televised Supershopping Sprees on the likes of CNN, *Good Day New York*, and NBC and think that each shopping experience requires hours of work for a big payoff. It doesn't, and with a bit of time, patience, and persistence, you can realize 50%–65% savings on a consistent basis. It may not be the 95% savings you'll see on my televised broadcasts (now viewable on my website www.CouponQueen.com and You-Tube), but then again, we don't always have Oprah or Regis looking over our shoulders!

The Five Steps

My five-step Supershopping System is an easy-to-follow program that will teach you everything you need to know to become a Supershopper like me. The steps are based on my thirty-seven years of experience in the field and thousands of supermarkets shopping trips.

Follow each step carefully, and when you have completed this book you will be ready to hit the supermarket to save more than you ever could have imagined.

The five steps are these:

Step 1: Get into the Mindset

Step 2: Choose Your Store

Step 3: Use Coupon Power

Step 4: Shop Smart

Step 5: Aggressive Saving

In this section we'll discuss the key points behind each of the steps. In each subsequent chapter you will learn exactly what is involved in each, see how to go about doing what is necessary to achieve your goal, and find some important statistics as well as helpful hints from various sources (including, of course, your very own Coupon Queen).

So without further ado . . .

Step 1: Get into the Mindset

According to the Promotion Marketing Association's Coupon Council, over 300 billion manufacturers' coupons are issued every single year, and that figure keeps rising. That's $350 billion in total potential savings. And of that number, guess how many were redeemed by today's supposedly savings-savvy consumers.

The answer: only 3.25 billion coupons, for a grand total of under $2.6 billion, which is little more than a 1% redemption rate and less than 1% of their total value!

Think about that. Why, if Americans today are so bent on saving money, are they ignoring this windfall of free cash? Some of the common reasons I hear—like not believing the savings are worth the effort, feeling embarrassed about using coupons, not having enough time, not fully understanding where to get coupons—all boil down to one simple factor: the shopping mindset. You must embrace the belief that everything can be bought at a discount. That's right: *everything!*

Ask yourself: "When I go shopping, what am I thinking about?"

If your answer is, "Getting what I need and getting out as soon as possible," then you are missing out on huge savings that will likely make a big dent in your monthly bills. If you answer, "Trying to save as much as possible," then you may have the right attitude, but I bet you're not going about it the best way. Most people will shave money off their costs simply by cutting out items they once bought, eating less, or giving up their favorite foods. That's all well and good, but why go without when I can teach you how to buy all the groceries you need and love and still save money?

The first step in becoming a Supershopper is changing your mindset about how you spend money. Yes, this requires a shift in the way you think, but in the end, you will be happier and

> **The first step in becoming a Supershopper is changing your mindset about how you spend money.**

healthier once you realize how much more you can save at the checkout by spending smart as opposed to starving and skimping. Looking for the deals, comparing prices, swapping brands, trying new stores, checking flyers and magazines— all of these are measures you can take to get into the Supershopping mindset.

Another important part of this step revolves around my POP Blocks: *Plan. Organize. Practice.* The POP Blocks are the fundamental components of my program. With these three simple building blocks, combined with a change in your shopping mindset, you will have taken the first step in readying yourself for big savings.

Plan **ahead:** Knowing what you have to buy and gathering the materials you need—including your store flyer (printed as well as online) and coupons—are crucial aspects of getting ready to enter the supermarket. With the right materials and forethought, you can move on and . . .

Organize **yourself:** Getting your coupons together, making a usable filing system, and setting aside the proper amount of time for planning and shopping trips are a must before you can . . .

Practice **your routine:** The more you work on the system, the easier it will become and the less time it will take.

It may take some time to get used to the ideas and practicalities of Supershopping, and at first it may seem frustrating. Oftentimes, the steps I will cover may seem counterintuitive to you. It may require a bit of research and time before you can figure out where in your neighborhood you can find the right resources like coupons, refund offers, and the like. You may find that you can do things faster without the system, and maybe you can—but faster does not always equal cheaper.

The great thing about my system is that anyone can do it, and once you start, you will find what works best for you and develop a modified version of the system on your own. You may find, for example, that you need a bit more time in the store than what I will recommend or that you are not interested in using the digital media I will cover later on. My goal is not to force you into a rigid set of rules to which you must adhere or you will fail miserably; rather, I want you to use my advice to find a comfortable means of saving as much money as possible, depending on what your schedule will allow. In time, this "personal Supershopping System" that you devise for yourself will become part of your life, a fun and integrated hobby that will do what most hobbies do not: save you 50% off your grocery bill every time you shop.

Step 2: Choose Your Store

Choosing the right store can make a major difference in your grocery bill, sometimes as much as 30%, simply because some stores offer more sales on a frequent basis or have better overall bargains. And then, of course, there is the question of coupon acceptance and refund offers, which we will delve into later.

Now, when I say "your" store, I don't want to give the impression that I am referring to only *one* store. In fact, a staple of my system is knowing when to switch stores and cut off loyalty to the one you are in the habit of frequenting. Supermarkets exist to make money, and while customer service may be one of the tools they use to keep your business, saving you money is not one of their objectives. If you want to cut your grocery bills, you have to go where the savings are.

I'm a creature of habit. I know how tempting it is to pick your "usual" and stick with it. But it's not economically viable. Don't fall into the trap, thinking your loyalty will be rewarded.

By learning all you can about the ins and outs of the supermarket game, you will be better equipped to tackle your shopping trip. Hopefully the facts I will teach you will convince you to leave the comfort of your corner deli or local market for a thriftier choice. This is not to say, of course, that you cannot develop relationships with the people at your favorite stores or prefer one to another. But your first priority should be savings.

Step 2 is all about understanding what kind of markets are out there: from organic and specialty food stores to larger markets, from mom-and-pop minimarts to giant grocery chains, and everything in between. All of these places have their perks and, depending on your diet and where you live, there are advantages and disadvantages to each. But most consumers don't know what those are. In step 2, we will cover everything the supermarkets don't want you to know about their industry, and I'll teach you how best to utilize your alternatives in saving the most money.

Step 3: Use Coupon Power

This vital step in the Supershopping system is about more than knowing what a coupon is and how to use it. Most of us are aware of what coupon clipping entails and how to redeem

> Creating an easy-to-maintain coupon filing system is essential. You don't want to waste time rummaging through a stack of coupons to find the one you need.

a coupon when buying a product. When I wrote my previous edition, this was not the case. Most people back then were completely unaware of what coupons did and where to find them, and today, according to the Coupon Council, around 94% of American consumers use coupons at least occasionally.

Here, I will spend less time focusing on the basics of coupon use and will expand our scope to things like (1) where the best and the most coupons are located, (2) how to organize them, and (3) the "tricks of the trade" that separate the Normal Shopper from the Supershopper.

As I stated before, only about 1% of all coupons issued are ever redeemed. Why? Because people are unaware of them. Manufacturers want you to use coupons. They are a marketing and publicity tool the corporations use to keep you coming back for more. That doesn't mean, however, that they are easy to spot. Knowing where to find coupons is not common among most average consumers, and as a result, few shoppers get past that first hurdle and never take advantage of the millions of "free" dollars floating around out there. Before you can "use Coupon Power," then, you must know where to find those lovely little slips of paper!

As stated briefly in step 1, organizing is a huge part of being an active and successful Supershopper. Creating an easy-to-maintain coupon filing system is essential. You don't want to waste time rummaging through a stack of coupons to find the one you need. Part of step 3 is learning systems that can further help you organize and be more efficient with your time.

Ever heard of Grocery iQ? Digital shopping lists? SMPs? I explain a plethora of coupon tips and secrets that can add extra savings onto your available coupons. Also, there have been huge advancements in technology that have made it easier to find and use coupons for just about every single product on the market. Knowing what you need and having coupons is only half the journey. Using new technology and lesser-known coupon tactics—which I will teach you—is the second half of that journey, and it will make a huge difference in your bill.

Step 4: Shop Smart

Along with new technology have come new advancements in the ways supermarkets help you save. Things like store loyalty and rewards programs and better scanning systems, for example, can make your shopping experience more enjoyable and easier.

Step 4 brings us into the grocery store itself. Now that we have gotten ready, made our lists, chosen the right store or stores, and organized our coupons, we are ready to journey into the lion's den itself and shop.

I am often asked, "This system sounds great—but how do you do it?!"

In this section, I will not only take you on a sample shopping trip, guiding you step by step, aisle by aisle through the store, but I will also tell you about all of the many additional tools the supermarket itself provides to you, the customer.

Coupons and rebates come, for the most part, from the manufacturer, the big corporations that package food and ship it out to local groceries. The supermarket has its own savings systems in place to keep you coming back to that particular store (although we will only do so when it is to our advantage, not to theirs, right?). By knowing which stores offer which programs and deals, we will be better equipped to shop smart and save big.

I have made hundreds of televised appearances in which I took a "Supershopping Spree" with a TV crew following behind me, showing the step-by-step process of how I navigate the grocery store. The physical direction you follow, the order in which you put products into the cart, even the level your eyes should be at to realize the biggest savings—all of these are important when shopping in the store. Supermarkets want to force you to buy impulsively and spend more than you need to, and I'll show you how to recognize their tactics and shop like a Supershopper.

Drugstores and other retailers have started using rewards programs, but many people fail to take advantage of these deals because they don't want to carry around a handful of store cards with them every time they shop. Or they do carry them and end up never using them. Step 4 will teach you how to manage your cards and use them to their full potential, earning you points for other products, freebies, and even vacation trips, while at the same time saving you money.

Step 5: Aggressive Saving

Did you ever think that you could actually *make* money by being a smart shopper? Most people don't. The idea of refunds and rebates is beyond most people's scope, and for good reason: they're not always easy to find. But they're out there.

Step 5, the final part of the Supershopping system, can be considered the "extra mile" the true Supershoppers among us will go to realize maximum dividends. It is also one of the things that separates my system from all the others out there and truly

> **Step 5, the final part of the Supershopping system, can be considered the "extra mile" the true Supershoppers among us will go to realize maximum dividends.**

makes Supershopping a way of life that can change the way you shop forever.

Most other programs rely heavily on quick gimmicks designed to save you fifty cents here or a buck there. The Supershopping system takes no more work or intelligence than these, but through routine and practice, it will help you save over half your grocery bill each year and make you potentially thousands of dollars back from the manufacturers. This is what we Supershoppers call "aggressive saving"—taking that extra step to make money from the groceries you buy through refunds.

A refund (or rebate) is money the manufacturer mails you after you've bought a product. You fill out a form and gather together the "qualifiers"—for example, a specified number of proofs of purchase (which we will delve into later)—and you send them in to the manufacturer. Several weeks later your check arrives; oftentimes the amount you can get back adds up to almost the full purchase price of the product!

If you get into the habit of refunding consistently, you will realize dividends of thousands of dollars every year. That may not be enough to support a family, but it certainly helps pad your savings account! If you spend $150 per week on groceries, or $7,800 per year, a 50% savings will net you $3,900. Add another $1,000 in refunds and you are almost $5,000 richer. Who couldn't use $5,000?

Premiums follow a similar concept, except instead of cash

back you get free or heavily discounted bonus products, such as T-shirts, tote bags, and mugs. These make great stocking stuffers or Chanukah gifts at the end of the year.

There are endless "aggressive saving" tactics Supershoppers employ to go that extra mile and get a nice "bonus" throughout the fiscal year. And the perks do not arrive on a yearly or even a monthly basis. With my system, refunders will receive checks and premiums *daily* while still having plenty of time for their jobs and family.

So there you have it: five fun and easy steps that will turn you into a Supershopper like me and the millions of others the world over who have adopted my system. Whether you are a stay-at-home mom, a full-time employee, or a student looking to save money, my system can help you as it has helped so many others. All you need is the willingness to read ahead and boldly go where other Supershoppers have already gone. The road is laid out for you—you just have to ask yourself, "Am I willing to change the way I look at my spending so that I can live the way I want, eat what I want, and buy what I want, but still save money?"

I can see no reason why you wouldn't. It's easy. Follow me. I'll show you how.

STEP 1:

Get into the Mindset

••

Wake Up and Smell the Savings!

PRICE INCREASES ARE with us for keeps. The reasons for this are debated constantly by everyone from the professional economist to the teenage checkout clerk, but the point remains: as long as supply-and-demand is king, prices will always be on the rise.

Some blame the farmers. Others blame the retailers. And still others point to the countless middlemen in between. All of these take their cuts, of course, but the unkindest cut of all is taken by those who bear none of the responsibility and yet shoulder almost all of the burden of supermarket inflation: you and I, the consumers.

My Supershopping system is unique in that it uses the food industry's own strategies as levers to loosen its grip. The tenets of Supershopping are neither complicated nor revolutionary. What they say, essentially, is that if you want to come out ahead at the checkout counter, you have to play the markets' own game—only play it better than they do. You can beat them, but only if you use the ammunition they give you.

CHANGE THE WAY YOU SHOP

·········

As we will discuss in the next chapter, grocery stores are for-profit entities. Their sole goal is to make money, and they rely on consumers to make that happen. They want to keep their customers coming back and they will do what it takes to make that happen. This includes offering you tons of ways to save when you go shopping. The first step in becoming a Supershopper is knowing how to identify these methods and being on a constant lookout.

I've said it before and I'll say it again: redemption rates for coupons are low. People are busy, or intimidated, or confused as to how to properly save at the checkout. But the Supershopper knows that it is actually quite easy to buy products at a discount; almost every product available can be purchased for less than its selling price.

Thus, you must now alter your mindset when it comes to the way you approach the grocery store. Look at the endeavor in terms of *opportunity cost*: in other words, getting the most bang for your buck. If you simply race into the supermarket, buy what you need at that moment, and race out, you will overspend and miss out on potential savings.

When we go to the market, our first impulse is to buy what we know. Product loyalty can be very detrimental to the Supershopper; it promotes a passive shopping attitude and pigeonholes us into a buying niche that will end up costing us. Most products, despite what their labels claim, are relatively similar in nutritional content and taste. If you want to save big, you have to learn to think outside your traditional box. This means going for whichever product is cheapest (and we will look into how to determine "cheapness" of a product throughout the book). Shopping around and taking your time is an important aspect of gearing your brain into this new shopping pattern.

> **If you want to save big, you have to learn to think outside your traditional box.**

I understand that many of us have products and brands we "cannot live without," and I am sensitive to that. My family, too, has a few "nonnegotiable" items, such as Honey Nut Cheerios and Skippy peanut butter. Again, this may be one of the areas in your "personal Supershopping system" that you have to figure out. In my case, since the items are nonperishable, I can buy more than one when I find a great sale, so I don't have to sacrifice my savings.

How often do you shop? Whenever you need an item? When you happen to be near the store? Or do you have a regular, regimented schedule ("I shop every Wednesday evening no matter what")?

None of these tactics works for the Supershopper. Shopping by impulse or convenience will not net you the greatest results, and even if it seems like you're being efficient, you're wasting a lot of time. On the other hand, blindly following a strict schedule will prevent you from getting deals only available at certain times and will not result in your getting the products you truly need.

I recommend shopping approximately once a week, at a time when you will not feel rushed or stressed. Make sure you have appropriate time before your shopping trip to make a list and look through your house for items you might be running low on. Enter the store with a set idea of what you need so that you can avoid impulse buying, but be willing to change your list if different products happen to be on sale. If you know in advance that certain days have the sales you want, try to plan to shop on those days. My local store's "super specials" seem to coincide with the first few days covered by each week's sale flyer, so my shopping is geared toward these days.

OPENING YOUR EYES

·········

The most common reason the average shopper doesn't take advantage of the billions of dollars in grocery savings is that he or she is unaware that they exist. If not that, the average shopper believes they are far more trouble than they are worth. After all, one might think, why should I hunt coupons and go to all that trouble for a few cents off my next bill? To this I make two counterarguments: (1) we are *not* talking about "a few cents" here and (2) it isn't nearly as difficult as you think.

Take my recent shopping trip to Dominick's in Chicago. I bought $232.32 worth of groceries for $15.40—a savings of 93%, which included $46.11 in Dominick's Fresh Values savings plus $170.81 in manufacturer and Internet coupons, for a total savings of $216.92. Still think coupons aren't worth the trouble?

We are, as I mentioned earlier, talking about savings of 50% or more off your monthly grocery bill, savings that total well into the thousands by year's end. The truly dedicated Supershopper can save even more!

All it takes is a positive attitude and a bit of patience to transform yourself from a Normal Shopper into a Supershopper.

When was the last time you scanned the aisles for a good deal? Not just the products at eye level, but those above and below as well. Do you automatically go for the product with the lowest number on the price tag? How detailed and organized is your grocery list when you enter a store, and what kind of ammunition are you walking in with?

For the Normal Shopper, the answers are typically "Never," "Always," "Not at all," and "What ammunition?" But the Supershopper knows the right answers!

It's time to open your eyes! Savings are all around you—you

just need to know where to look. Next time you receive a store circular in the mail, don't just throw it out! Save it, look through it, and pinpoint the products that interest you. When you make your next shopping trip, do a bit of research. Consider it "Supershopper boot camp." We're putting you in training to become a more aware consumer, but the process has to start with you.

When I say research, I'm not talking about reading books (besides this one) or going to libraries. I'm referring to market research. You know the products you and your family eat. The wonderful thing about Supershopping is that you don't need to drastically alter your lifestyle or eating patterns to be successful at it. But you do need to learn flexibility.

Set aside some time for yourself in the supermarket on one of your next trips and, instead of just grabbing the products you are used to, look around at your options. How do the prices of your favorite brands compare with those of other brands you have never tried? Does one store you frequent consistently offer lower prices on a certain type of product, like canned vegetables or breakfast cereal? Where are the best selections to be had? Recently at my local A&P in Eastchester, New York, Edy's brand ice cream was on sale, two for $6.00. Since the regular price is $5.99 each, that's a 50% savings. Not bad, until you consider that three weeks ago the same Edy's was reduced to $1.99 each, a 67% savings, at Stop & Shop. Now *that's* the time and place to buy. Knowing the best price for all of your items will increase your savings dramatically.

Don't be embarrassed about bringing a calculator into a store with you and figuring out which size of product gives you the most bang for your buck. The same goes for a pad and pencil. Make notes on the products you buy most often, keeping track of the highest and lowest prices you find across each brand and throughout each different store. If others shoot you looks, remember: you will be the one smiling when the cashier totals your bill!

The supermarket is one of your best resources. In the cereal aisle, check the packages. You're sure to find Kellogg's offering a free T-shirt, a camera, a Matchbox car, or savings on other products. Recently, in the Fareway in Des Moines, Iowa, at least six pet food packages were offering 25% more in product. These are manufacturers' bonuses that don't increase the selling price:(pet food always yields a wealth of savings). How about the frozen food aisle? Not long ago I discovered a Tombstone pizza offering up to $15 off your electric bill. These are all in addition to the coupon dispensers, register coupons, and end-of-aisle displays. The lesson here is awareness.

THE POP BLOCKS

The fundamental principles of step 1 of the Supershopping system revolve around my POP Blocks: Plan. Organize. Practice. With these tools at your disposal, it becomes infinitely easier to head into the supermarket and make your savings.

Plan Ahead

Most modern-day consumers have a million and one things on their plates that they have to worry about on a day-to-day basis. Shopping for the necessities is often the last on their lists, and thus it is always done as a last-minute chore or spur-of-the-moment inconvenience. For the Supershopper, this method is detrimental to the very concept of shopping, as it promotes those passive shopping habits I mentioned earlier. Without proper preparation, both mentally and physically, there is no way to succeed at the grocery store.

The first step in the planning process, now that we've

made the commitment to becoming a true-blue Supershopper, is to generate a well-thought-out shopping list. Look through your house and figure out what products you are running out of. With many products, especially nonperishables or items your family uses often, it does not hurt to stock up if the sale is good, so keep that in mind as you make your list. If you still have a bottle of apple juice but your son goes through a bottle in three days (as mine does!), you may as well add it to the list.

What most shopping systems don't tell you to do is to organize your list into categories—not by brand or product name—but by grocery aisle. Since you've already done your "store research," you have probably noticed that grocery stores typically follow the same (or a similar) layout design, with frozen foods, dairy, fruits and vegetables, and meats around the perimeter, and canned goods, grains, paper products, etc., on the inside aisles. Once you know what products you need to buy, organize them into categories the way the supermarket does. After the first time, this will become much easier since you will already have the template in place for future shopping trips. It's a good idea to create a computer document with your basic list—things you need every week—and add weekly specials and buy-one-get-one-free offers (BOGOFs). This saves both time and energy. Stouffer's frozen mac and cheese was a BOGOF recently. Because it's a frozen item, two can sit in my freezer just as easily as one. But there are times when BOGOF deals are not practical. When lettuce was touted this way, I knew I couldn't use both heads before they went bad, so I passed this offer up. Common sense and space availability will dictate when these specials make it to your list. I also decide what produce to buy based on seasonal availability. Check out my sample shopping list on page 25.

Why go through the trouble of creating a list, you may ask? Two reasons: First, a well-organized list makes it easier to map out your route in the grocery store and pinpoint your items without getting sidetracked. The more distracted or aimless we are, the more we will repeat aisles or wander through areas we don't need to, and this inevitably leads to impulse buys and wasted time. The second reason is that, as we will discuss momentarily, our coupons will *also* be arranged in similar categories, so when we are comparing our grocery list to our coupon file in step 3, the process will take half the time.

Organize Yourself!

All the planning in the world won't amount to anything if you aren't organized. Unfortunately, this is usually the part of the system where most people start getting nervous, and understandably so. Organizing is hard for some people, but don't worry—my system will guide you through the process, making it simple and straightforward.

First, you should pick up a coupon file. A simple accordion-style envelope will do, but make sure it is compact and can fit a lot of flat slips without exploding. I have a similar one to mine on my site: CouponQueen.com. There is nothing quite like trying to corral hundreds of tiny coupons that have erupted from a poorly kept file! Many of the better files come with an elastic band that encircles the envelope to help keep it sealed tight. Just pick something that works for *you*!

Once you have a file, put in tabs for each coupon category (as we mentioned earlier). We will discuss in detail the best way to organize your coupons in step 3. For now, just make sure you have a solid filing system in place.

Susan's Shopping List

Baking

- 5 lbs. Domino sugar
- 5 lbs. Gold Medal flour
- 2 Duncan Hines cake mixes, any flavors

Beverages

- 1 2-liter Dr Pepper
- 1 2-liter Coke
- Mott's 64 oz. or 8-pk. apple juice

Canned Goods

- 15 oz. Green Giant cut green beans
- 20 oz. Dole sliced pineapple
- 8 oz. Folgers instant coffee
- 2 15-oz. Del Monte vegetables, any variety
- 3 5-oz. Bumble Bee solid white tuna

Condiments

- 7 oz. Wishbone dressing, any flavor
- 2 15½-oz. Ragú sauce
- 2 7-oz. Seven Seas dressing
- 18 oz. Welch's grape jelly
- 64 oz. Crisco oil
- 48 oz. Hunt's ketchup

Dairy

- 2 6-oz. Dannon yogurt, any flavor
- 1 12-oz. Kraft Singles
- 1 64-oz. Tropicana orange juice

- 1 gallon milk—check weekly sale
- 1 dozen eggs—check weekly sale
- 4 10-count Pillsbury biscuits

Frozen Foods

- 2 lbs. Ore-Ida potatoes
- Green Giant frozen corn, any variety
- 2 Green Giant frozen vegetables, any variety
- Birds Eye Little Ears
- Kashi frozen entree, any variety

Health and Beauty

- 32 oz. Listerine
- Reach toothbrush
- 6.4 oz. Colgate toothpaste
- 12-pack Kotex napkins
- 60-count Band-Aid bandages

Household

- 100 oz. Era liquid
- 32 oz. Spic and Span
- 42 load Cheer
- 50 oz. Palmolive dish detergent

Meat

- 2 lbs. any beef—check weekly sales
- 3 lbs. any chicken—check weekly sales
- 1 Oscar Mayer Deli Creations sandwich

Packaged Goods

Quaker instant oatmeal, up to $4

2 Post cereals, any variety

Bread—check weekly sales

1 Jell-O Singles, any flavor

Paper Goods

1 Bounty, any size

2 Scott tissues, any size

1 Foil or Boutique Kleenex

2 Viva, Big Roll

Produce

Carrots

Lettuce (Dole 50¢)

Celery

Apples or other sale fruit

Organizing yourself also means organizing your time. Make sure to set aside a solid thirty minutes to an hour for every grocery trip, at a time when you will not feel rushed. Also, outside of shopping trips, you will probably want to devote a few minutes each day to looking through the latest sale flyers and online offers, since now more than ever these sales are changing every day. I usually allot about four to five hours a week to review flyers, cut coupons, send in for refunds, and work on my shopping list. This may take a bit more or less time for you, but four to five hours is a good estimate.

Four to five hours may seem like a lot of time to spend, but not when you consider a savings of $5,000 or more a year. That said, I do most of this during downtime, like while watching TV at night or waiting for my meal to finish cooking or the clothes dryer to stop. I never take time away from the important stuff.

Solid organizational skills will help you feel more confident when you enter the grocery store. When you know what you need and where to find the coupons for each product, you won't have to worry about fumbling around when you are in the market or at the checkout. Plus, with an organized grocery list like the one described above, you won't be doing any aimless wandering or impulse buying!

> As with any system, the hardest part is getting started.

Practice

As with any system, the hardest part is getting started. Hopefully you are encouraged enough by the plethora of savings opportunities out there to take advantage for yourself and begin saving thousands of dollars each year. I promise it will happen if you follow the Supershopping method, but patience is a virtue.

Each time you create a Supershopping grocery list, cut out your coupons, and hit the store with your "ammunition," it will become easier and easier to save because you will have developed a routine. Routine leads to habit, and before long you will find yourself cutting time (not to mention dollars!) from your shopping trips without even thinking about it.

STEP 1:
GET INTO THE MINDSET
....

In this chapter we have been discussing the first step of my five-step system: getting into the mindset of saving big, keeping an eye out for savings opportunities, and changing your shopping habits. Let's review the key points of step 1.

1. Think outside your box.

Normal Shoppers fall into the routine of buying what they know without thinking twice about the potential for savings. Start doing some "market research" by shopping around at different stores and learning what a "good deal" on your favorite products truly is.

2. Plan on shopping for an hour about once a week.

Impulse shopping leads to more money spent, so hold off on your trip until you have generated a solid list of items, not just one or two here and there. Remember, the more time spent in the store throughout the week, the more random impulse buys you will make.

3. Keep your eyes peeled.

Being alert means not throwing out store circulars that are sent to you in the mail or walking past in-store flyers or ignoring coupons inserted in magazines. Be active, not passive, in your pursuit of savings.

4. Remember the POP Blocks.

Plan ahead by making a concrete shopping list, arranged in alpha order by category as the items are laid out in the grocery store aisle. Keep your files and lists *organized* for when you prepare to go into the store. And *practice* the system often to develop a healthy shopping routine.

So, are we ready to move on to the next chapter? You've embraced the necessary mindset and are prepared to use it-next let's find out which supermarket is right for you!

2

Choose Your Store

··

Winning the Supermarket Game

THIRTY YEARS AGO, when *Cashing In at the Checkout* hit the stands, grocery shopping offered relatively few choices. Today, there are a mind-boggling number of places we can go to get our food and basic household necessities. So how do we pick? Do we even *need* to pick?

In a lot of cases, there is no right answer; everyone's shopping habits gear them toward a different grocery alternative. As a Supershopper, however, it is vital to know the advantages and disadvantages of each type of store and choose the store or stores that will both reflect your personal shopping habits and provide you with the biggest savings. I have my own personal favorite picks, but I am not one to think that my way is the only one that could work. You have to learn the differences before you can make the choice for yourself.

Before we can effectively discuss picking the "right" store for you, we should look at the history of grocery shopping.

• • •

THE EVOLUTION OF THE SUPERMARKET
·········

Mom-and-Pop Shops

Before there were gigantic supermarkets dotting virtually every street corner, and "big box" stores such as Target and Wal-Mart competing for our business, people did much of their shopping at small mom-and-pop stores. These markets were generally owned by a neighborhood resident whose entire family put in long hours to run the store. The prices were not competitive and the selection was small, but this was, more or less, the only option available to shoppers. Low in technology and selection, mom-and-pop shops had severe disadvantages.

But these local stores served a unique purpose. They were plentiful, with one in almost every neighborhood. The owners knew all their customers. Often, credit was extended to customers without the aid of credit cards. It was a comfortable way to shop.

Unfortunately, competition from larger chains started to push these mom-and-pop stores out of existence several decades ago. Chain stores had a buying power that small shops could not equal. And because of the long hours and low profits, the children of these shop owners usually wanted better jobs and didn't want to carry on the family business.

Now, except in some of the larger cities where space is at a premium and in small towns that lack giant chains (which are few and far between nowadays), mom-and-pop stores are a phenomenon of the past. Those that do still exist, however, are great for quick shopping trips or last-minute buys, as they are easy to get in and out of and not laden with thousands of choices. But because of their small size and limited budget, these shops can rarely afford to offer major sales, nor do they usually accept coupons. Therefore, what you see really is what you get.

Co-ops and Specialty Stores

In the 1970s, a new genre of shopping was created in the form of co-op grocers, which were generally small retail markets. They combined the comfort of mom-and-pop stores with the collective buying power of some of the larger chains. The members paid a minimal yearly fee to join, donated a few hours a month for the benefit of the co-op, and then shared in the discounts offered to the group. Some of these co-ops still exist today but they find it difficult to compete with chain stores. I won't spend much more time in this book on co-ops as they are relatively quite rare.

Specialty stores also carved out a niche for themselves at around the same time, but unlike co-ops, they continue to thrive today. Some of the more popular specialty stores are Trader Joe's, Whole Foods, and Stew Leonard's. In general these are smaller, easy-to-navigate markets that offer mainly their own brands, while still providing a similar product variety as other stores. The prices are competitive and the quality of the food is excellent. At Trader Joe's, one of my favorite items is the one-pound smoked salmon for $11.99. That's less expensive than any of my other local stores. Their avocados sell four for $3.99, also a great buy with equally good quality.

All of these specialty stores have large sections devoted to health and organic foods, a category that has risen in popularity in recent years. With the advent of new organic food technology, people have begun flocking toward these more healthful, environmentally conscious, and animal-friendly options. Often, health and organic foods are more expensive. For example, chicken costs an average of $1.19 per pound, so a four-pound chicken costs about $4.76, versus $3.99 per pound for organic chicken, which is $15.96 for the same size. Still, many Americans believe it is more important to pay top dollar to know just where their meat and dairy come from, and that, of course, is a personal choice. And as of late, I've noticed more competitive pricing on these specialty items especially produce, cereals, granola bars, and dairy since almost every variety of store carries an organic section, and manufacturers are getting on this bandwagon too.

One disadvantage to shopping at specialty stores is their lack of coupon acceptance and store sales. As I just mentioned, they offer almost exclusively their own product brands, so manufacturers' coupons are useless at these markets. In addition, as with mom-and-pop shops, they can't really afford to offer any products on sale. Still, I love stores like Trader Joe's since they do offer great selection and prices when my local supermarkets are dry on sales or discount offers.

Supermarket Chains

Supermarkets can trace their history back to August 4, 1930, when Michael Cullen introduced the nation's first ever supermarket in Queens, New York. He dubbed the store King Kullen after his son's drawing of a man sitting on top of the world. Michael Cullen probably never imagined how he would change the shopping experience of future generations.

Today, supermarkets can be found in every corner of the United States and in many countries around the world. They spurred the growth of mass merchandising and encouraged innovation, leading to the advent of the shopping card and the bar code.

Supermarket chains have increased in popularity, technology, and size, particularly over the last thirty years. I remember going to my local Daitch Shopwell in the 1970s and handing the clerk my coupons. She added up my coupon savings on a brown paper bag used for packing the groceries and handed me the cash. There were no electronic cash registers figuring out my deductions. The register was really just a large calculator. The clerk punched in the cost of each item and the machine gave her the total. It didn't even tell her how much change I needed to get back when I paid. She had to do the math herself!

The advent of new technologies has made checking out at the supermarket a whole lot simpler and quicker. Perhaps the greatest innovation was the creation of the bar code, or Universal Product Code (UPC). The first UPC-marked item ever scanned at a retail checkout (it was at a Marsh Supermarket in Troy, Ohio, on June 26, 1974) was a ten-pack of Wrigley's Juicy Fruit chewing gum.

The use of UPCs on products enables the industry to create an automatic inventory system. The UPC has a series of printed bars and sometimes numerals, with no letters or other characters. It is widely used in Canada and the United States for tracking items in inventory. While most stores, big and small, now scan the UPCs of the products on their shelves instead of manually counting them up, supermarkets go several steps further. For example, each time a product is scanned at the register the store is able to adjust its inventory count. And when products go on sale, the change is made by computer; no errors should occur at checkout. Bar codes are also printed on store and manufacturer coupons. The purpose is to speed checkout and to eliminate incorrect coupon deductions by use of sophisticated computer systems.

> The loyalty cards that most major chains offer to shoppers, simply by signing up, are useful to both consumers and the supermarkets.

The loyalty cards that most major chains offer to shoppers, simply by signing up, are useful to both consumers and the supermarkets. For the shopper they eliminate the need to cut out coupons from the store flyer—a big advantage for shoppers who often forget their coupons at home. Loyalty cards also offer big advantages for the supermarket. Each shopper creates an individual profile of preferences based on his or her purchases. This is of great benefit to the supermarket in ordering the correct quantity of products. Consider this: an average supermarket has upwards of fifty thousand different products. That's a lot of inventory. Knowing its clientele's preferences aids the store in maintaining an efficient and cost-effective business. And some of these savings are passed along to the customer.

Have you ever seen those coupons that come out of a separate machine or on the back of the cash register receipt as you check out? These are called Catalinas. They, too, are linked to your shopping habits. I often buy soy products, so I receive Catalina coupons for new soy items when I check out. When I buy detergent, a competing brand issues a checkout coupon as well.

Now we can even do our own checkout. My A&P has four self-checkout lanes that also accept coupons. It's a big money saver for the supermarket and reduces wait time at the checkout.

· · ·

Warehouse Stores and Supercenters

Target and Wal-Mart, are known as supercenters that sell not only clothing and household products but also groceries. The selection of grocery products is not as varied as at the traditional supermarket, but the prices seem to be better on many items. I have noticed a recent trend of families doing almost all of their shopping at these supercenters since the variety and prices are right. And sometimes, as opposed to some warehouse stores, supercenters often do accept manufacturers' coupons and, as opposed to specialty stores and co-ops, they offer sales quite often.

My problem with supercenters is that they encourage impulse buying simply because there is *so much* available. Unless you need clothing, camping equipment, and sporting supplies in addition to your simple grocery needs, it's best to avoid supercenters so that you can focus on the grocery shopping. Also, unlike supermarkets, supercenters almost never double or triple coupon values, a savings strategy that can often mean the difference between a 30% and a 60% savings for you.

Warehouse shopping is another milestone development that has grown in scope in the past twenty-five years. The first Sam's Club (a Wal-Mart company) opened on April 7, 1983, in Midwest City, Oklahoma. BJ's Wholesale Club was next, opening about one year after Sam's. The warehouse concept includes a membership program that requires a yearly fee. Buying is done in bulk. Shoppers pack their own purchases in leftover packing boxes and in general manufacturers' coupons are not accepted.

In recent years, however, Costco, another warehouse, has been issuing a manufacturers' coupon book, valid only in Costco. BJ's also has its own manufacturers' coupon book, but in addition it has begun accepting a variety of manufacturers' coupons. If BJ's sells a four-pack of Kleenex tissues, you can use a coupon on each box—a big plus for the shopper. Some warehouses also issue their own store coupons. These coupons often expire within only a few weeks, so while this is better than nothing, it forces you to shop during a certain window of time, before the coupon's expiration date, which puts you at a disadvantage. You may not need a particular perishable item during that window but may feel compelled to buy it "just in case" since the expiration date is fast approaching. This sort of "time crunch" shopping is not unlike the way many electronics or major appliance stores sell their furniture by saying, "This sale will only be around for another week, so hurry up and buy now!" Supershoppers are *never* pressured into buying something they don't need just because a coupon is set to expire!

However, the biggest disadvantage for me is the bulk-buying concept. For nonperishable goods, this works fine. But for cereals, frozen items, dairy goods, and produce, I find that freshness is lost, and often dairy products and produce go bad. One other consideration in bulk shopping is space limitations. Living in a house affords me many areas of storage. But for three of my sons living in apartments in Manhattan, space is an issue. Common sense and your rate of usage should help in customizing your purchases.

My sons have become very ingenious at storing items. Lots of paper goods, like paper towels, go under the sink where the back corner is usually empty; extra canned goods, pastas, cereals, and snacks go into the upper hard-to-reach kitchen cabinet; and finally a shelf added to the bathroom vanity holds additional tissues, cleaning items, and toothpaste. As they say, necessity is the mother of invention.

I don't use the warehouses as my primary store, but warehouse shopping does fill some shoppers' needs, and if you need a huge miscellany of other nongrocery products, there is no reason to completely avoid these stores.

SO WHERE DO YOU GO?

·········

I recently conducted a comparison shopping survey for each of the types of stores I just discussed (except co-ops, since they are so few and far between), analyzing the price differences between over fifteen products from store to store. This was done over a year of shopping in different stores throughout the country, and taking the average price for each product.

What I found was not terribly surprising: the major warehouses and supercenters, overall, had the lowest prices and offered the most bulk purchases. Supermarkets and specialty stores were in the middle, and mom-and-pop shops had slightly higher prices on most products but especially low prices on others.

I then went back to the exact same stores and looked at the exact same products, except this time I factored in sales and coupons. The change here was pretty remarkable: the warehouse and supercenters went from the top of the list to the middle, the specialty stores remained exactly the same (since they don't have sales or accept coupons), while the supermarkets dropped nearly 80% in overall price!

What's the lesson here? For the Normal Shopper, it makes the most sense to shop almost exclusively at supercenters and warehouses since the overall price is lowest at these places. However, for the Supershopper, the best alternative is to stick with the supermarket for all major shopping trips, since no other type of store will double or triple coupon values and have the abundance of sales that the supermarket has. Of course, there are definite merits to the other types of stores, and throughout the rest of this chapter I will outline exactly what these merits are.

COMPARISON SHOPPING SURVEY
(NO COUPONS)

GROCERY ITEMS	MOM & POP	SPECIALTY	SUPER-MARKET	SUPER-CENTER	WAREHOUSE
64 oz.Tropicana Orange Juice	5.29	2.99	3.79	2.74	2.51
½ gallon of milk	3.39	1.59	2.19	1.69	1.03
1 dozen eggs	2.79	1.79	1.69	1.19	0.82
5 oz. Dannon Yogurt	1.39	0.79	0.99	0.99	0.75
50 oz. Gain Detergent	11.99	3.99	4.99	4.29	3.61
12 oz. Maxwell House Coffee	5.79	5.99	3.29	2.89	2.53
64 oz. Wesson Oil	10.99	6.98	5.69	5.39	3.05
Kleenex Foil Tissues	2.79	0.99	2.19	2.24	1.32
Bounty Paper Towels	2.99	1.33	2.29	1.57	0.99
6.4 oz. Colgate Toothpaste	3.49	1.99	2.29	3.49	2.98
5 lb. sugar	4.69	6.59	2.49	1.97	2.35
Green Giant canned vegetable	1.79	0.89	1.29	0.99	0.88
5 oz. can Bumble Bee Tuna	1.99	1.49	1.59	1.49	1.25
Large Wonder Bread	3.19	2.49	3.19	2.49	1.59
Kellogg's Cereal	5.39	1.99	3.99	3.49	2.19
1 head lettuce	1.99	1.99	1.79	N/A	N/A
1 lb. of chicken quarters	N/A	2.99	3.99	2.99	1.99

Prices for specialty and mom-and-pop stores remain the same since coupons are not accepted in these stores.

Items at the specialty stores are all private label, similar to a supermarket's store brand. I shopped throughout the country, over a year time period. These are prices from a variety of different locations.

Because most of my experiences deal with the supermarket, I always take advantage of sales and double coupons. I find my savings the best here.

N/A: Not available

Comparison Shopping Survey
(With Coupons)

GROCERY ITEMS	MOM & POP	SPECIALTY	SUPER-MARKET	SUPER-CENTER	WAREHOUSE
64 oz.Tropicana Orange Juice	5.29	2.99	1.49	2.24	2.51
½ gallon of milk	3.39	1.59	1.59	1.69	1.03
1 dozen eggs	2.79	1.79	0.77	1.19	0.82
5 oz. Dannon Yogurt	1.39	0.79	0.09	0.51	0.75
50 oz. Gain Detergent	11.99	3.99	1.99	3.79	2.99
12 oz. Maxwell House Coffee	5.79	5.99	1.49	2.39	2.53
64 oz. Wesson Oil	10.99	6.98	2.99	4.39	3.05
Kleenex Foil Tissues	2.79	0.99	0.59	1.09	1.03
Bounty Paper Towels	2.99	1.33	0.49	0.85	0.89
6.4 oz. Colgate Toothpaste	3.49	1.99	0.09	1.49	2.24
5 lb. sugar	4.69	6.59	1.49	1.47	2.35
Green Giant canned vegetable	1.79	0.89	0.09	0.99	0.88
5 oz. can Bumble Bee Tuna	1.99	1.49	0.77	1.29	1.25
Large Wonder Bread	3.19	2.49	1.49	1.23	1.59
Kellogg's Cereal	5.39	1.99	0.49	2.99	1.79
1 head lettuce	1.99	1.99	0.09	N/A	N/A
1 lb. of chicken quarters	N/A	2.99	1.99	2.99	1.99

Warehouse stores: adjusted for size-15 cans of only green beans $13.25, single can .88
Warehouse stores: Cereal 49 oz. box $6.69, difficult storage and freshness compromised.
I adjusted price since the average cereal is 16 oz. I divided by 3 to get $2.19 for 1 box.
Warehouse stores: some accept coupons or issue their own coupons—prices reflect this.
Supermarket and supercenter prices reflect sales, coupons and double coupons.
You may be able to get better prices at the supercenters, but this is what I found on my trips.

Aside from price, there are a number of other factors to consider. Your choice of store type will depend on the following (some of which I have already discussed):

❖ Proximity to home and cost to get there (gas)
❖ Selection and variety of products
❖ Average costs of your top items
❖ Whether or not they take store and manufacturers' coupons and they double or triple coupons
❖ The loyalty programs and how they fit your needs
❖ How often they have in-store sales (and if those are on the products you buy)

Where is the best place to shop, and how do you pick the best store? First, think about your own shopping needs. If you generally do not shop for a large family and you do shop about once a week as I recommend, supercenters and warehouses are not for you, since they will encourage you to purchase tons of various nongrocery products, and to purchase them in bulk. Plus, they are a nightmare to navigate.

My biggest factors are in-store sales and coupon acceptance. Typically, smaller chains and mom-and-pop shops cannot afford to lower their costs and put items on sale, nor do they often accept coupons. When they do, they are almost never doubled, let alone tripled. The smaller stores are great for a sense of comfort and ease, but don't forget: they are businesses looking to make money. Don't think for one second that by patronizing a local shop you are doing a community service. Do *yourself* a service and get the best bargains you can!

Supermarkets, in my opinion, offer the best choice of all these store types, and by sticking with larger supermarkets you cut down on travel time and gas expenses. You will still probably

> **Here's my rule of thumb: pick your favorite supermarket chain and use that as your primary store.**

need to have two or three supermarkets in your area to fill all your shopping needs on a monthly basis, but that's better than having ten stores to go to. Besides, if you find yourself near a mom-and-pop shop or warehouse, you can always enjoy the benefits of those stores as well. But we're talking about your *typical shopping trip* here, the place you will go most often for most of your necessities.

Here's my rule of thumb: pick your favorite supermarket chain and use that as your primary store. Always have a couple of reserves in case the sales at "your store" are not matching up to your coupons or if they don't carry the product or products you need. I choose my local A&P because I love the sales, the coupons, the variety and product selection, and the multitude of promotions, especially double and triple coupons and now online coupons. My savings are by far the best here and I have done comparisons over and over again to verify my findings. However, as I said, I do still frequent most of the other types of markets as well, and here's why.

I started shopping at Costco because my father, with whom I did much of my shopping in the 1980s and '90s when Costco was just beginning to become popular, would drag me there to taste the samples. We would say, "We're going to Costco for lunch." Of course, Costco's purpose wasn't to serve us lunch, but to entice us to try some of its products, purchase them, and shop some more. And the strategy worked. Along the way I found some very well-priced products and I continue to shop there on occasion. BJ's has been a good attraction as of late because of their multiple and stacking acceptance of coupons. On a three-pack of Colgate toothpaste, you can use three Colgate coupons.

Trader Joe's (a well-known specialty store) is another favorite of mine because of the quality of its products and the low costs. This is never a replacement for the supermarket, just a supplement to my regular purchases.

The supercenters offer great buys, they do accept coupons, and they have weekly sales. But the selection is limited, and fresh items such as meat are prepacked. It's a convenient one-stop-shopping trip since if I want, I can purchase lawn furniture, clothing, and groceries in one fell swoop, but again, this is not the main source of my grocery shopping.

Mom-and-pop stores are abundant in New York City, the home to three of our four children. I do stop in for the occasional loaf of bread, container of milk, or batch of flowers, which, by the way, are very reasonable. Three bunches of carnations, lilies, or mums average $9 or $10, actually cheaper than the supermarket.

With all this in mind, let's start looking in depth at the place where you will spend most of your grocery shopping time (and the place that the remainder of this book primarily focuses on): the supermarket.

THE NATURE OF THE SUPERMARKET

There's a rumor going around that supermarkets exist to sell food.

Actually, selling food is a secondary matter to them. The reason they exist is the same reason every other industry outlet exists: to make money. Supermarkets do not stay in business by overseeing whether or not your pantry has enough crackers or cat food to meet your family's needs; they stay in business by getting you to spend money, and the more of it the better.

Supermarkets don't do this out of malice or contempt for the consumer. On the contrary, most supermarkets maintain quite a healthy respect for their customers and are more than willing to steer you toward their cheaper and more convenient products. But this does not mean you should confuse them with philanthropic organizations. No store manager in his right mind is going to offer you a bargain that does not also show a healthy profit for the store.

Supermarkets are like huge casinos, matching their wits and luck against each other to see which one will reap the lion's share of profits. The store that comes in first in this race is the one that succeeds in getting the most shoppers to spend the most money in the smallest amount of time.

Now, I realize there are some major distinctions between casinos and supermarkets. For one thing, there is an immediate tangible consolation for those who prefer to put their money down at the checkout counter rather than on the blackjack table: the groceries they come away with. Even if you've just dropped half your paycheck in the till, you do go home with those cookies and asparagus tips.

There is another major difference between casino games and the supermarket game. In all casino games, there is a mathematical certainty that, over the short as well as the long run, the house will win and the player will lose. In other words, the odds are always stacked against you in a casino. If you figure out a way to beat those odds—if you come up with a system to beat their system—they simply ban you from further play.

This is not the case in the supermarket. There is no mathematical certainty attached to any one marketing technique; as a result, you can't say that the odds are stacked against you. In fact, the markets give you plenty of opportunity to manipulate the odds in a way that would just get you thrown out of games in Las Vegas. Unfortunately, very few shoppers take advantage of these opportunities.

Furthermore, the supermarket house rules do not bar the introduction of a system. If, as I have done, you come up with a system of beating the house every time, they do not ask you to leave. I can't imagine an Atlantic City or Las Vegas casino doing anything at all for the customer whose intention is to beat the house. Supermarkets, on the other hand, almost beg you to hit bingo whenever you shop, and the Supershopper, using my system, can hardly fail to do so.

Supershoppers know the house rules and how to use them to their advantage, while Normal Shoppers fall easy prey to these very rules—because they're unaware of the high-powered marketing techniques designed to make them leave the store with dozens of things they hadn't thought they wanted. If you've ever come home with six cans of tomato paste instead of four simply because they were on a "three-for" sale you'll recognize what I mean. Let the Normal Shopper spend too much on things she doesn't need.

WHEN TO FORGET LOYALTY

Now that I've determined the best type of store to shop in, my actual choice for the week will vary. First, I check to see which stores double or triple the value on manufacturer coupons. These promotions will vary from time to time, so it's important to check the print or online flyer for details. Next, I review the supermarket flyers to see who's offering the best sales for my purchases. Included in this review are any special promotions.

For example, for a six-week period, my A&P is offering between 5% and 15% off the total when I spend $200–$400 on a shopping trip. However, Pathmark, for a thirty-day cycle, is offering $10 off my purchase of any frozen items amounting to $30 or more. I decide on Pathmark because it also has all the frozen items on sale, as well as sales on cereal, eggs, coffee, and crackers, all of which I need. Both supermarkets are within a five-mile driving radius: another criterion of mine. I almost never go to more than one market in a typical week, but I have done so when the sales and promotions were too good to pass up.

Thus, supermarket loyalty is a consideration for the five or six in my area, but my final and most important decision is based on savings. Which supermarket can save me the most? After all, we're all in this to "win the supermarket game" and become the best Supershoppers we can be.

Normal Shoppers practice a strange type of "loyalty," both to their favorite stores and to individual products within those stores.

A recent survey conducted by IBM indicates that in today's economy, more people than ever are giving up store and brand loyalty in favor of whatever product is cheapest. Now try to guess exactly how many of these "shifters" make up the total percentage. Probably a lot, right?

Nope, just 30%. Even when store loyalty is at an all-time low, seven out of ten people are still refusing to give up loyalty to their local stores or chains (according to the Coupon Council). And that loyalty is costing that 70% heavily.

In the era of the mom-and-pop store, store loyalty probably had a lot to do with friendship and real community feeling. In the age of the chain store, I can't see that it has to do with anything else but habit. And this habit can be extremely hazardous to your budget. Suppose the A&P down the street is running a special on hot dogs. Does it really make sense for you to pay $1 or $2 extra per pound simply because that A&P is not "your" store?

Loyalty in the abstract is an admirable quality, but loyalty toward a giant chain can very quickly turn into the love of being *en*chained. If you can't bring yourself to switch stores to take advantage of a sale two blocks away, you are stacking the odds against yourself. The minuscule amount of time you may save shopping a bit closer to home will hardly be worth adding a 15% or 20% surcharge to your shopping bill.

We all have our favorite markets, of course. I know I do. But if I see an attractive special advertised by a rival store, I become Benedict Arnold in a minute. Being on the lookout for which store is offering you the best odds this week is an essential part of my Supershopping system. No food store is out to do you any favors. You may have a friend in a produce manager here or in a butcher there, but each store as a whole should be judged on precisely those merits the stores themselves consider central: the quality of the merchandise and the price being asked for it. Don't forget: all of these stores, no matter how friendly or personable the staff is, are here to take your money. If you want to show your appreciation for a friendly staff, buy them a present at holiday time; don't bind yourself to their store to make them happy.

Remember that one of the delightful things about playing "market roulette" is that, if you don't like a store's odds, you can take your business elsewhere. In the casinos, all the roulette wheels are alike, but supermarkets vary widely, because they are part of a competitive free market system. Check out the competition. It keeps them on their toes, and you'll thank yourself for comparing.

The same thing goes for *product* loyalty. Again, most of us seem to have our favorite brands, and another unfortunate aspect of Normal Shoppers is that they often stick with those brands no matter how the prices soar. Brand-name loyalty makes no more sense to a Supershopper than loyalty to a particular store.

Look at the labels and you'll see that I'm right. The difference between one brand-name soap and another in terms of ingredients is often negligible, and since the big manufacturers should have no greater hold on your heartstrings than the big chains, why not buy what is cheapest?

Given the habits mentioned above, the Normal Shopper is sure to lose the shopping game. She sticks with one store, one line of products, and fills her cart with high-markup items because she hasn't prepared ahead of time.

Are you a Normal Shopper? I know I was until I discovered the system. What the system taught me was that I could take matters into my own hands. I could shop *rationally*, not impulsively. And I could win at their game.

All you need to shop rationally is a system based on an understanding of how marketing works from the seller's point of view. We have already covered some of the basics of this, as well as some of the drawbacks to each particular type of store. But we have left out one important factor: sophisticated and aggressive marketing techniques, techniques used to get you to spend more than you want to. To help you understand the principles of these ploys, I want to give you a few of the seller's unwritten rules.

This in itself will not ensure that you will be able to beat the seller's game. For that you'll need all the interlocking parts of my system. But it will give you a clearer idea about why you should be mildly suspicious as you shop, and it will tell you some of the methods supermarkets across the country use to keep shopping odds in their favor.

•   •   •

SUPERMARKETS:
CAPITALISM AT ITS FINEST

·········

Do you know what Maxwell House coffee, Nabisco cookies, Kool-Aid, Planters peanuts, Ritz crackers, Oscar Mayer hot dogs, and Jell-O have in common?

They are all produced by the same company, Kraft Foods. This illustrates a basic element of the modern food marketing system: extensive diversification under a few giant corporate umbrellas. The days of the small local company are fading fast. Today, nearly everything on your shelf has been made by one or another firm that figures someplace in the Fortune 500. Some of the big names to note, other than Kraft, are Campbell Soup, Kellogg, Land O'Lakes, General Mills, Procter & Gamble, and Dole.

This means that food has become big business, or "agribusiness," as the experts call it, giving an official linguistic stamp to what had been common practice for decades. Most of our groceries are produced by a few gigantic concerns, and virtually every one of them spends millions of dollars each year to convince you and me that their products are superior to all others. This can be a big boon for you as a shopper, who can use these

> Most of our groceries are produced by a few gigantic concerns, and virtually every one of them spends millions of dollars each year to convince you and me that their products are superior to all others.

ploys to increase savings, so long as you don't fall into their traps! Let's look into these traps and see if we can't increase our own awareness when it comes to shopping.

Advertising

All major manufacturers (and most smaller food manufacturers as well) spend millions, often billions, of dollars on advertising. For example, Procter & Gamble, the biggest moneymaker on "household aids," spends approximately $1.25 *billion* each year advertising its wares, according to TNS Media Intelligence. Kraft goes well beyond that, at nearly $3 billion per year in advertising. Twenty-five years ago, the entire food industry spent a total of only $6 billion. Between them, the two manufacturers mentioned above spend nearly the same amount as all of the food industry combined!

What does that mean to you? It means that somebody out there wants your dimes and nickels very badly. And it means that they are willing to pull out all the stops to get them.

This is a mixed blessing for the shopper. On the one hand, the intensive competition for your shopping dollar may tend to keep inflation in check by leading to price wars, special promotions, and the like. On the other hand, the enormous expense of making sure you remember Product X's name must be made up from somewhere, and generally that "somewhere" is in the price you pay for the product, as advertising costs are simply passed on to the consumer. Costs of advertising and packaging—which today is a special kind of advertising—now account for a very high percentage of the price of our groceries. This is item one to remember when you consider the supermarket game. Coupons are the only advertising medium that actually helps you save, so let's use them . . . and use them wisely.

New Products

Manufacturers believe that, in order to keep your attention from month to month, they have to offer you a constantly changing array of new products.

It's nice, of course, to have a new cereal to try each month, but again the result for the consumer is mixed. Not only does the high cost of bringing out all those new cereals get passed on to us (product development, consumer testing, package design, advertising, etc.), but the proliferation of new products pushes manufacturers to subject you to an overload of advertising and gimmickry in order to offset the sheer volume of choice. If there are only three coffees to choose from, advertising is a relatively simple matter. When the number of choices goes up to five or ten, novel ways must be devised to capture your attention.

Today's shopping choices are mind-boggling indeed. There are approximately 100,000 products available to shoppers today, and each grocery store has room for about 40,000 to 60,000. The number of new products swells each year, as more and more manufacturers are trying to keep consumer focus with "new" and "exciting" products, "low-fat" and "diet" options, and new flavors or twists on old favorites.

This is one reason why shopping at small local stores every so often is nice; the selection doesn't make your head spin! Still, you *will* find the best deals in supermarkets; you just have to know where to look and be aware that the best-advertised item is not necessarily the most cost-effective item.

In-Store Promotions

Most new products do just what most new businesses do: they never get off the ground. Each year, food retailers spend an

> **There are approximately 100,000 products available to shoppers today, and each grocery store has room for about 40,000 to 60,000.**

average of $956,800 per store on new products that fail, according to a study by the market research firm Linton, Matysiak & Wilkes. Most of these new products fail within their first few months. Only about 15% of them, in fact, ever make it into the second year's sales reports. As a result of this drastic attrition rate, manufacturers will do almost anything to get you to try a new item, and to keep on using it. In the markets themselves, store managers do their part to see that you remain convinced, and as a Supershopper you should be particularly wary of the techniques retail stores employ to promote new (and old) products.

Many store owners have learned a whole bag of psychological gimmicks to promote sales. We will delve into these in detail in chapter 4, but I want to introduce them briefly here. By cagily arranging their floor plans, by promising big bargains, and by using various pricing techniques, stores are able to boost sales significantly. These techniques, employed by virtually every chain store in the country, constitute the way that the supermarket game is played from the companies' side. If you are unaware of them, they can take as big a bite out of your paycheck as the national TV ads can by influencing you to buy unwanted products. If you recognize them where they occur, you'll find they can become one of the most fascinating parts of the game to outwit.

In-store promotion is the most widely used marketing gimmick, more so than all media advertising. The reason is obvious: as more and more people stop reading general newspapers and watching TV in favor of surfing the Web or reading special-interest magazines, manufacturers and retailers are finding it easier to reach people where they shop, not at home. Browsing a medium-sized market in Cedar Rapids, Iowa, I found upwards of one hundred different promotions, including coupons, in-package deals, on-package peel-off instant coupons, and great money-back refund offers; consumers can turn many marketing gimmicks into big savings. Open your eyes and smell the savings!

STORE BRANDS VS. NATIONAL BRANDS: THE MYTH REVEALED

So, we're right back in the supermarket aisle, flanked by endless rows of bold lettering and snappy pictures, all designed to convince you that This Brand, and no other, is best. Accepting that the supermarket, though it is surely no paradise, at least offers a wide choice and relatively fast service, you're faced with the common dilemma: which brand, out of the mad array, offers the best buy for the money?

Many shoppers are loyal users of one or another national brand and buy that brand year after year, certain that they always know what they're getting. But most shoppers stick with store brands, convinced that they're every bit as good as the national labels. Thinking they are saving money, the Normal Shopper is turning more and more to private-label store products, according to Frost & Sullivan. So which method is right?

Now, I can't tell you which brands to buy on the basis of which are "best." No studies have indicated that there is a very significant difference in "quality" between national and store brands. And the ingredients in most of these products are almost identical; take a look for yourself next time you hit the store. The results of a double-blind nationwide taste test released recently by Meyers Research showed that about half of consumers preferred the taste of store brands, and half preferred national brands, so clearly there is no real difference in taste!

Yet I buy brand names exclusively, and, in fact, a cornerstone of my Supershopping is that you must buy *only* the nationally advertised brands, leaving the apparently cheaper store brands for the less systematic bargain hunters.

Why do I insist on this? The answer is simple: money. In the long run, *the brand-name items are cheaper*.

Whenever I mention that Supershopping relies on brand-name shopping, I get incredulous stares. Somehow, people won't believe that you can actually save more money buying the "expensive" brands rather than the bargain lines. On one radio show, a woman called in to say, "That's just not logical! Surely you'd save more by sticking with the cheaper items." Paradoxically, you wouldn't. Illogical as it may seem, my system reaps its greatest dividends only when you buy the "high-priced spread."

There's a simple explanation for this. Although the store brands may have cheaper price tags, they have the great disadvantage of being produced by companies that don't have the means to promote them. That means that (1) you cannot use coupons to buy them, (2) no one will ever offer you a refund for buying them, and (3) they are almost *never* on sale. The combination of these three factors means that, over the long run, you will lose out by staying with the store brands.

Say, for example, that you're pricing a canned vegetable. The Green Giant brand is going for $1.79, while the same size in the store brand is only $1.59. Most shoppers would consider the store brand to be a better value.

But not the Supershopper. She has checked through her

coupons and come up with a 50¢ off Green Giant coupon, which right away makes the 20¢ higher item *30¢* cheaper at the checkout, at $1.29. In addition, the Supershopper gets a Green Giant label from this sale, and in a few weeks that label, combined with others, is worth another $2 in refund, so eventually she will have gotten the green beans free, and made 71¢ besides. We will talk more about refunds in step 5.

I don't have anything against store brands per se. There is a sameness about them, though, and if you like to vary it up a bit as I do, the lack of new products in the store-brand line can get to be boring. As we discussed above, the national brands can afford to introduce tons of new products every year (with matching promotions!), but not the store brands. I don't think there's a great difference in quality, and if I thought store brands were truly (rather than only apparently) cheaper, I'd probably switch to them myself.

According to the Private Label Manufacturers Association, store brands average about 25% lower on ticket price than the nationally advertised brands. This seems like a big difference, but when you consider that I save approximately 65% on my grocery bill by sticking with brand names, it's not so big after all. Using my system leaves me a comfortable 40% margin for profit with coupons alone. Refunds add even more to my profits, sometimes as much as $2,500 per year.

In addition, making money by buying the big companies' brands gives you, as any Supershopper will testify, a satisfying feeling of having beaten the corporate giants at their own game. Sure, they'll still jack up the prices next week—and faster than the store brands—but they'll also offer a host of new coupons and refunds in compensation. With a little dedication to the system, you can learn to outguess them and turn each new increase into a dividend.

STEP 2:
CHOOSE YOUR STORE
·········

We've spoken a lot in this chapter about the nature of grocery stores and how you can choose among them. There is a lot to remember when it comes to the types of stores out there and the differences between them, and it's not easy to keep straight. So now that we've discussed the ins and outs of the food industry, let's review what we've discovered:

1. Know the advantages and disadvantages of different types of stores.

The smaller the store, the smaller the selection and higher the price. Medium-sized stores offer the best sales and most regularly accept coupons, while larger stores have the best selection and lowest overall prices (before coupons and sales).

2. Establish criteria for your store choice.

Things like proximity to home, frequency of sales, coupon acceptance policies, and average prices are all good things to keep in mind when making your selection. Try to keep one primary store in mind and have several backups in case your store is not having strong sales during a particular week.

3. Look out for marketing ploys.

Supermarkets are here to make money. Knowing the advertising gimmicks they employ will help you save time and money when you are making your way through the supermarket. End-of-aisle displays, flashy signs, and deals like "10 for $4" can be marketing tricks. Legitimate sales are advertised in the store's weekly flyer. Keep the lowest price in mind, and you'll know the difference.

4. Remember, loyalty matters in war, not shopping.

There is no good reason to stick with a certain store or brand. Follow the sales. Even though sales generally cycle through brands and stores, they are often unpredictable. Be flexible and willing to change.

5. Stick with national brands.

Yes, in the short term, store brands are cheaper. But with the introduction of coupons and refunds, which we will discuss in the next few chapters, you will discover that national brands always net you the most savings, since those companies can afford to offer dividends in the form of coupons and refunds.

All right! We're mentally prepared and organized with our list and we know what we need to buy. We've found the store or stores that are right for us. Now it's time to start saving with coupons!

STEP 3:

Use Coupon Power

....

Feel the Power

COUPONS WERE INTRODUCED in 1895 by Postum Cereal Company (what is now C. W. Post). Of course, these were coupons that advertised *pennies* off a product, not dollars like they do today. Still, the concept of using store or manufacturer coupons to shave money off your grocery bill is well over a century old. Yet only about 15% of us regularly use coupons, and 80% are sporadic coupon users, according to recent studies by Scarborough Research.

The big question is: how come we're throwing away all this free money?

Most people are not actively avoiding coupons. They do, however, feel that it takes too much time and effort to hunt them down, and they honestly wouldn't know where to begin if they decided to start being active coupon users. This attitude always makes me shake my head in bewilderment and disappointment. We want to save money. Manufacturers and retailers want us to save money. Why aren't we saving money?

The toughest part about Supershopping is getting started,

> Only about 15% of us regularly use coupons, and 80% are sporadic coupon users, according to recent studies by Scarborough Research.

and I promise you, if you follow the steps in this book, it will take you virtually no time at all to start saving big and making a habit out of it. So let's get right to the heart of the matter: coupons and why you want them!

COUPONS: A STAPLE OF SUPERSHOPPING

As I mentioned in step 2, Supershopping mandates that we only buy national brands. Yet I've also made it clear that there are cheaper alternatives out there, between store brands and bulk purchases from warehouse stores like Sam's Club, Costco, and BJ's. So how do I reconcile the difference?

The answer is coupons.

There are some interesting statistics associated with couponing that show something about both the food industry's eagerness to make it easy for us to buy (and save) and the Normal Shopper's strange reluctance to take them up on it. The statistics show, for example, that although the manufacturers are spending more and more money each year issuing coupons, the American public seems no more anxious today to cash in on the companies' offers than it was when the first coupon was printed well over a century ago. Coupons, it seems, are still a little mysterious to many of us; we use them only on a haphazard, almost incidental basis.

> Since C. W. Post issued the first 1¢ off coupon in 1895, coupons have functioned as the most visible and most widely distributed promotional scheme in the industry's whole bag of tricks.

Actually, there's nothing at all mysterious about them. Since C. W. Post issued the first 1¢ off coupon in 1895, coupons have functioned as the most visible and most widely distributed promotional scheme in the industry's whole bag of tricks. Almost everyone has used a coupon at one time or another. Often you don't even need to buy products to acquire them, because the companies mail them to selected "occupants" throughout the country.

To really profit from Coupon Power, you have to approach couponing as a daily, enjoyable habit. That's the only way you can start cutting your register tape in half every time you go to the store.

Coupons are by far the most vital piece of the Supershopping puzzle, so it is crucial that you understand both where they come from and how to use them effectively. There are two types of coupons, or "cash-offs," to keep in mind: manufacturers' coupons and retailers' coupons. The difference is simple.

Manufacturers, the big Fortune 500 companies, create thousands of products each year, and they will often issue coupons for these products that are redeemable at *any* store that accepts coupons as a general policy. Store or retailer coupons, in contrast, are issued by a particular store in its weekly flyer and they are usually only redeemable at that particular store.

Fortunately, many supermarkets will accept *both* types simultaneously (this is called "stacking"), and some stores will even accept store coupons from competitors' stores as a means of beating their prices. This works as a double whammy (in the good sense) for the consumer—it drastically cuts your cost for national brand products, savings that you would not realize with store-brand products, because the maker or the store almost never issues or accepts coupons for those.

For example, a box of Kellogg's Corn Flakes is running at $3.89 for a box at your local A&P. A similar store-brand cereal costs only $3.69. At first glance, the store brand is the better deal. However, you, a budding Supershopper, smartly checked the store flyer and your own personal coupon organizer and found both a retailer cash-off at A&P for 50¢ as well as a manufacturer coupon from Kellogg's for an additional $1 off. The result? A total of $1.50 off the corn flakes, or $2.39, $1.30 cheaper than the store brand!

And that's just the tip of the iceberg.

Throughout this chapter we will discuss other coupon and savings incentives and then get into systems for organizing and finding coupons. When you're done with this chapter, you'll be amazed by how much you have been missing out on!

WHY COUPONS ARE "WORTH IT"
·········

How many times have you opened a box of cereal and thrown away a 75¢ off coupon offer inside because you figured it was "just too much trouble keeping track of those things"?

How many times have you ignored your local market's weekly flyer because you thought it wasn't worth it to clip coupons just to save a few cents on your bill?

How many times have you saved a coupon for months, then handed it to the checker only to discover it had expired?

If you're like I was before I developed the Supershopping system, you've done all of these things many times. American shoppers, bargain conscious as they have had to become in recent years, still have barely scratched the surface when it comes to saving with coupons. Perhaps they think there is something slightly shameful or "cheap" about using these manufacturers' dividends, or that using them is just another form of skimping. One common image of the dedicated coupon clipper, I suppose, is that of the slightly batty shopper who ties up the checkout line for an hour rummaging through twenty pounds of paper in her pockets. Coupon clippers seem to be thought of as a bit eccentric—as if there were something crazy about taking your savings seriously.

And this is why $350 billion in coupons are discarded throughout the average year.

That's just like throwing away money. If shopping can be considered a game, then coupons are truly "winner's chips."

Approximately 148 million Americans are current active coupon users, says the Coupon Council. The term "active coupon users" refers to individuals who use at least one coupon on their weekly grocery trip. Given that the population is currently hovering around 310 million, this means that less than 50% of us use coupons on even a more-than-occasional basis. Less than half of those use coupons regularly.

The issuing of coupons, however, has been on the constant rise since the 1960s, when the first "coupon boom" began. At the beginning of the 1960s, for example, only about 350 manufacturers were using coupons, at a total value of $191 million. By 1976 both these figures had doubled, and the number of coupons issued was up to 46 billion. By 1984 they upped that to 160 billion, with a new face value of $35 billion. By 2007, the Coupon Council further reports, that number had skyrocketed to over *302 billion coupons*, for a grand total of $387 billion in redeemable CPG (consumer packaged goods) manufacturers' coupons! And none of this is taking into account the many store-issued coupons.

To give you an idea of how fast coupon issuance is growing currently, let's look at the jump from 2006 to 2007. CPG manufacturers increased their number of coupons 16% in that year alone, with a total face value increase of 9% (from $337 billion to $367 billion)—remember, in just one year! This trend has continued in recent months, and with the advent of online coupons (which we will discuss later in this chapter), that number is jumping with unprecedented speed.

Yet of the $387 billion worth of coupons issued in 2008, only $2.8 billion was redeemed (2.6 billion coupons out of an available 302 billion). That's less than 1%! Americans may be thought of as wasteful, but to throw away $385 billion in *free money* . . . now that's just silly.

Why the shoppers of America are not cashing in on this bonanza, I don't know. Obviously a fear of the unknown, or of looking silly in the supermarket, or ignorance of the cash windfall and how to take advantage of it all play a part. I *do* know that I'm doing my part to see to it that the redemption rate rises above the going average of less than 1%. If you're a Supershopper, you'll do your part as well. The manufacturers are continuing to increase the volume of coupons issued each year, begging us to try their products by offering us substantial savings if we do. I consider it my public duty to take them up on their offers. And some of you have taken this public duty seriously too. According to the *New York Times* coupon use has risen every quarter since 2009 making it the first year of rising coupon use since 1992.

Not only the manufacturers, but the stores themselves want you to do it. Manufacturers allow stores to charge hefty handling fees in addition to the face value of the redeemed coupons. As a result, many individual stores are reaping their own bonanza on coupons, as the big companies pay them in some cases 8¢ or even 12¢ per coupon they handle. Say you use ten coupons on your next trip (I would hope you would use more, but ten is a nice round number), the store you shop at will *earn* $0.80–$1.20 for your patronage and also be reimbursed for the face value of the coupons themselves. If $2.6 billion in coupons were redeemed throughout 2008 alone, and the stores got 8¢ for handling each one, that's an annual gross profit for the stores of $208 million!

Coupons are still the firms' principal way of getting you to try new products, and coupons benefit them from an economic standpoint as well. Thus, if you are worried that by walking to the cash register with a file full of coupons you will dismay the checkout clerk or store manager, you couldn't be more wrong. Unless a store manager has totally forgotten where his own best interests lie, he won't resent reimbursing you for couponing.

And don't feel bashful about using coupons in a store that doubles coupons. The extra money the supermarket gives you beyond the face value of your coupon is absorbed by the store as advertising and promotion expenses. If the store's managers did not consider doubling an effective means of encouraging you to use their store, they wouldn't offer it.

There is some evidence that the redemption of coupons is on the rise, as a survey conducted by comScore, a leading online researcher in consumer trends, indicates. But it's not rising nearly fast enough to keep up with the increase in production. In fact, 2008 was the *only* year since 1992 that the redemption rate did not decline (nor did it increase), and actually did increase in 2009, and while redemption rates are strongly linked to economic trends, even in the worst of recessions people are not taking full advantage of their own Coupon Power.

EMPOWER YOURSELF

How much can you save with coupons?

It would be misleading to suggest that you will be able to realize 95% or even 85% savings every time you go to the store. I have been cutting coupons (and bills) for over thirty-five years. I have a huge file of coupons available to choose from, and I am able to use both my experience and this large stack of "winner's chips" to make an extraordinary killing at the market. On a weekly basis I can't do that, because my backlog of coupons would soon be depleted, and I'd be down to using coupons only for things that I didn't really need. And that is something that a Supershopper never does.

On my weekly shopping trips I generally save between 50% and 65% of my bill. Cutting the bill in half is about normal. In other words, I'll buy $60 worth of goods, and shell out only $30. This is not as fantastic as what I do on a typical Supershopping Spree for a television show, but it sure beats paying full price.

And, you must remember, I make that 50%–65% savings not just occasionally, but *every time I shop*. Over a year that really adds up. Last year, Steve and I estimate, we put over $5,000 in the bank as a result of couponing and refunding alone.

When I do my Supershopping Sprees for local TV shows and newspapers, my savings are more impressive. Naturally, prep time for these trips will take much longer than my normal trips, but they net me savings of up to 95%. As a quick example of how these sprees work, let me describe how I prepared for one of my most recent trips, at a Shoppers in Alexandria, Virginia.

Preparing for this trip was no small process. First, I went to my coupon file. This is simply a long, bulky accordion-style envelope in which I keep, in categorical followed by alphabetical order, all the clipped coupons I now have on hand, including cents-off coupons, free coupons from manufacturers, and printable coupons. Before every shopping trip, I flip through them to see what items on my list I can get for a reduced price.

Then I checked through the local Alexandria papers until I found a store in the area that did two things: (1) advertised a fair number of good sales on the products I wanted and (2) offered double value for coupons. We will discuss this more in a moment.

I found a store a couple of miles away from our hotel that fulfilled both requirements, so I adjusted my list in line with its particular sales and told ABC the location so the producers could clear the filming with the store manager. Needless to say, he was delighted to have us.

And I was delighted, too, when the trip worked out so much better than any of us—including myself—had expected. The look on the face of the show's producer when he heard the final total would have made the junket worthwhile all by itself—even if I hadn't saved $150.10, 92% of my original total.

I have taken similar shopping trips for newspapers, radio stations, and television programs from New York to San Francisco, and I will continue to do so until people no longer use money to buy food.

On one such trip for ABC News in New York, for example, less than $10 got me $148.16 worth of groceries. In Milwaukee, at Sendik's Food Market I paid $15.98 for purchases worth $132.54; that's a savings of 88%. In Philadelphia, taking advantage of doubling at a downtown Acme, I bought $211.70 worth of merchandise—and the store only got 42¢ of my money. One of my favorite shopping trips was in the Chicago Dominick's, where I met a long-time subscriber to *Refundle Bundle*, Ben Salkin. We shared stories, photos, and saving tips. It was certainly the highlight of my trip.

So step 3 of the system is definitely "worth it."

SHOPPERS.

YOUR Satisfaction is
My Pledge to you!

3801 Jefferson Davis Hwy
Alexandria, VA
Store No: 2649
Phone:703-518-4711

12:35:51

02/22/10

GROCERY

```
1 @ 2/ 3.00                           1.50 F2
HAWAIIAN PUNCH RE  1480064600         1.00 F2
RICEARONI SPNISH   1530043053         2.69 F
GOLD MEDAL FLOUR   1600010610         3.69 F
KSHI HNY ALMND BA  1862703001         1.49
DELMNTE CREAM COR  2400016301         1.49
D/M SWT PEAS       2400056515         1.49
D/M SWT PEAS       2400056515         1.4
D/M W/K WHT CRN L  2400056669         6.
FOLGERS COFF       2550000088         2
ZPLOC STORAGE BAG  2570070985         2
HUNT'S KETCHUP     2700038354
PALMOLIVE 25FL     3500043530
VIVA PAPER TOWEL   3600019208
VIVA BIG ROLL 1CT  3600019213
1 @ 2/ 4.00
KLNX TISSUE ASST   3600028201
1 @ 2/ 4.00
KLNX TISSUE ASST   3600028201
OLD WRLD MARINARA  3620000400
OLD WRLD MARINARA  3620000400
CHEER LIQUID DTGN  3700011033
CASC DISH DETERGN  3700018867
BNTY PAPER TOWELS  370002135
DOLE PINAPLE SLIC  38900001
1 @ 2/ 5.00
W/B BALSMIC VING   4100000
1 @ 2/ 5.00
WISHBONE DRSNG 16  410002
SHPRS WHITE BREAD  411130
1 @ 2/ 7.00
POST HBO CEREAL    4300
1 @ 2/ 7.00
POST HBO CEREAL    430
MAYO 30 48
```

```
                           77933SC      -1.00
Vendor Coupon    51862700001MC         -3.69
Vendor Coupon    52100012000MC         -2.99
Vendor Coupon    52400000050MC          -.50
+Double Coupons  52400000050DC          -.50
Vendor Coupon    52400000050MC          -.50
+Double Coupons  52400000050DC          -.50
Vendor Coupon    52400000050MC          -.50
+Double Coupons  52400000050DC          -.50
Vendor Coupon    52400000050MC          -.50
+Double Coupons  52400000050DC          -.50
Vendor Coupon    52400052101MC         -1.49 F
Vendor Coupon    52550075300MC         -6.99 F
+Double Coupons  52570010055MC          -.55
Vendor Coupon    52570010055DC          -.55 T
Vendor Coupon    53500050001MC         -2.50
Vendor Coupon    53600030001MC         -3.29
+Double Coupons  53663220032MC          -.75 FS
Vendor Coupon    53663220032DC          -.23 F2
Vendor Coupon    53700016001MC         -7.49
Vendor Coupon    53700032100MC         -5.99
Vendor Coupon    53700045200MC         -2.19
Vendor Coupon    53700051500MC         -5.48
Vendor Coupon    54300051400MC         -1.69 FS
Vendor Coupon    54800110001MC         -3.99 FS
Vendor Coupon    56414431001MC         -4.49 FS
Vendor Coupon    57192117201MC         -3.49 FS
Vendor Coupon    57261399282MC         -2.00
Vendor Coupon    57764400001MC         -1.99 FS
Vendor Coupon    58660010001MC         -1.15 FS
Vendor Coupon    58660010001MC         -1.15 FS
Vendor Coupon    58660010001MC         -1.15 FS
```

```
******** VOID * TRAINING MODE ********
********* DUPLICATE RECEIPT **********

          SUBTOTAL               12.95
          VA 5% TAX               2.44
          VA 2.5% TAX             2.65
     TOTAL          18.04
********* DUPLICATE RECEIPT **********

Cash         T TENDER           18.04
Cash         CHANGE               .00

          NUMBER OF ITEMS           63
MANUFACTURER COUPONS      54  130.83
Store/Dbl/Triple Coupons  13   19.27

YOU SAVED A GRAND TOTAL OF       150.10
THAT IS A SAVINGS OF
                                    92%

------- FSA Total $3.45 --------
Use your Health Care spending card here.
Items ending with "H" qualify for
          FSA purchase.
```

WHERE TO GET COUPONS

·········

The first thing the novice couponer needs to know is where to get them. There are numerous ways to obtain coupons. Here are the most common:

In the Store

Many coupons come in specially marked packages at the store. The most direct way that manufacturers choose to acquaint the shopper with new products or special offers is to enclose within their products coupons either for a second purchase of the same product or for one of their other products. Many coupons are printed right on the outside of the package. Others are inside. When a coupon is enclosed in a package, it will be advertised on the outside. Naturally, the Supershopper prefers to buy products with coupons rather than those without.

This is assuming, of course, that the price difference between the special package and the regular package is not so great as to neutralize the attraction of the coupon. If you're choosing between two national brands, a $1.69 carton of pasta with a 60¢ off coupon inside really costs no less than a $1.09 carton without the coupon—so you may as well, in such a case, take the lower-priced brand and leave the coupon for a later date.

Peel-off or "hang tag" coupons, found right on the carton or bottle, are a slightly different breed. These provide instant savings on your *current* purchase. Other instant coupons may be found in red blinking dispensers throughout the aisles of many stores; these are generally associated with a marketing company called SmartSource. "End cap" displays—special shelving placed near the beginnings of the aisles—are another location, boasting yet more coupons, inside many stores. "Tasters"—the people who offer food samples to shoppers—give out coupons, sometimes for a free package of the product. Finally, the checkout offers coupons with the printing of your register receipt; these are known as catalinas.

The supermarket is surely giving you the tools; you just have to learn to use them.

In Magazines and Newspapers

Newspapers carry not only national CPG manufacturers' coupons, but also"in-ad" coupons: that is, cash-offs being offered, usually for one week only, by individual local stores. Obviously, both can save you money. Checking the midweek and Sunday papers will give you an idea of where you can save the most with local coupons each week. In fact, the Sunday paper is still the single best source for coupons (53% of coupon-collecting households get their coupons from the Sunday newspaper, according to Scarborough Research).

At the same time, you can clip the national coupons, which are good for a much longer time. Remember here that the savings are not only for supermarkets, but also for pet supply, office supply, book, and hardware stores. The flyers and their deals can almost form their own newspaper.

As for magazines, nearly every large-circulation magazine in the country features grocery and household coupons on a regular basis. The best sources are, of course, the "women's magazines," which you generally pick up at the supermarket checkout—*Family Circle*, *Woman's Day*, and so on. But coupons also appear almost every week in nearly every general-interest periodical.

ASSORTED COUPON SOURCES

STORE COUPONS

Subscribing to a lot of magazines, therefore, is one way to ensure your get a steady supply of coupons. But subscription is not the only path. A more ingenious and frugal way of getting magazine coupons is to trade them with your friends. I have an arrangement with my neighbor Bonnie, for example, whereby she gives me all her dog food coupons and I give her all my coffee ones. You can also simply ask friends to pass along to you whatever coupons they don't use.

Doctors' and dentists' waiting rooms are another good source. I always carry scissors with me when I go to the doctor, and I generally manage to find at least three or four cash-offs I can use. This may seem a bit indelicate, but not when you remember that, if some savvy Supershopper didn't remove these coupons, they'd soon end up in the trash, like money thrown away. Doctors' offices sometimes also provide coupons left behind by salesmen who want to target their market. Recently, my local dermatologist had $15 in coupon offerings on Aveeno and Eucerin face and hand creams in a smart handout. And my family dentist gave me not only samples of Colgate toothpaste but also savings on Crest. I couldn't smile much on my way out, but I was happy knowing I had added to my cache.

There are other methods, less well-known and underused. One method is to keep an eye out for neighborhood paper drives and offer the sponsoring organization a small fee for letting you clip coupons from their collections before they bundle them for resale. Also, local recycling centers have magazines bundled neatly for easy coupon access.

You can probably come up with other ways to fill up your coupon file from magazines. In general, just remember that almost all magazines contain some cash-offs. Keep that in mind whenever you thumb through one. (I'm not suggesting, of course, that you snip your way through library or bookstand copies.)

From Home Mailers

I don't suppose there's anyone in the country who hasn't at one time or another received a letter addressed to "Resident" or "Occupant." Manufacturers periodically send out advertising circulars to whole neighborhoods of people, and frequently these "direct mailers" or "home mailers" contain coupons.

Coupons received in the mail seem to be very popular with the American shopper. While the overall redemption rate for coupons is well under 1%, the rate for home mailers can go as high as 25%, according to the Promotion Marketing Association. Naturally, this makes direct mailers popular with manufacturers as well, and for the past several years they have consistently increased the number of flyers-with-coupons they send out. So if you haven't received a home mailer lately, your turn may be coming up.

The nice thing about home mailers is that you don't have to put in any effort to obtain them. As long as you're an "occupant" (and most everybody is an occupant of something), they'll eventually come to you.

You can speed up the process, however, by becoming an active refunder (see step 5). As soon as I sent in for my first cash refund, I found that I had mysteriously gotten onto several manufacturers' mailing lists, and I started receiving home mailers on practically a weekly basis. Providing information to manufacturers directly via their websites (see the section below on printable coupons) is another way to ensure a constant supply of mailers.

Home mailers, according to some, come under the heading of "junk mail." While I am no big fan of unsolicited advertising, I can't quite bring myself to think of coupons that save me up to $2 on a single item as "junk."

But then Supershoppers are biased: we're in favor of saving money.

Through CouponQueen.com

While newspapers and magazines and home mailers provide a large quantity of coupons, they may not supply enough of the specific coupons that you are using weekly. Realizing this problem, I set out to do something to remedy the situation. The result was the Select Coupon Program, now online at Coupon-Queen.com.

The main purpose of my program is to simplify the process of acquiring coupons and provide the largest selection of coupons in a single location. We gather tremendous quantities of coupons from thousands of suppliers throughout the country, people who cut coupons from their magazines and local newspapers. Now shoppers in Des Moines, Denver, Peoria, and Oklahoma City or any community where coupons are scarce have the option of finding their favorite coupons with the click of a button.

The program sorts and categorizes national brand coupons consisting of close to one thousand selections at any given time. Thus, consumers are able to look online at our "coupon catalog" and pick out the coupons they need. Becoming a member is simple, and once you're on board with us, all you have to do is let us know which coupons you would like to receive and we will send them to you.

As a coupon supplier, the process is reversed: scour your local newspapers, magazines, what have you, and clip everything you can. Send the coupons to us and we will reward you for every one you mail in. The coupons we get from our suppliers, for the large part, make up the database from which we send our members their choice of thousands of different coupons. It's a wonderful give-and-take that reinforces the community aspect of couponing and saving that I love so much.

I have been busily updating the program's website over the past few years to incorporate other helpful additions for our members. Hundreds of coupon and refund postings on the discussion board add to your savings. Blogs offer great money-saving tips. The Deal of the Day will greatly increase your savings with typical freebies, rebates, and coupon specials. The videos give a step-by-step idea of what a Supershopping trip looks like. And this is just the beginning. I have already developed a way in which Supershoppers can use the site to help them organize their grocery list, search their local store flyers for sales, and find the best deals available for their favorite products, all from my one site! Be sure to keep up with me online at CouponQueen.com for more updates, great saving tips, and incredible offers. And don't forget Twitter and Facebook, you'll find me at Coupon Queen.

In later chapters, we'll discuss other ways in which Supershoppers like yourself can help others throughout the country in their quest to save at the supermarket. If you would like to find out information about the program, don't hesitate to check us out on the web at www.CouponQueen.com. Don't forget: we're all in this together.

As Printable Coupons Online

Printable coupons are really catching on, and I do use these coupons on many occasions. They are different from digital coupons, which we will discuss later, in that these are physical coupons one can print directly from home and bring to the store like any other cash-off, while digital coupons are uploaded directly to a mobile device.

Data from comScore indicate that 27 million people visited coupon sites in October 2009, up 33% from 2008. This is still a relatively low number, considering that only about 18% of

> **All of the printable coupons on the Web originate from only a handful of sites. The most popular and accessible are Coupons.com and manufacturers' websites.**

coupon users have turned to printable coupons as another means of acquiring them. But given how new this technology is, that is a surprisingly fast growth. The number of coupon-related Web searches increased by 100% from January to September of 2009 in the United States alone, and by 42% internationally. So it's certainly not just a U.S. trend!

All of the printable coupons on the Web originate from only a handful of sites. The most popular and accessible are Coupons.com and manufacturers' websites. Almost *every* other site that has printable coupons gets them from one of these sources. This means there is no need to waste your time on too many other sites.

Personally, I like Coupons.com because you can access multiple manufacturers' coupons from a single source, and the site doesn't require a lot of personal information to sign up. Coupons.com has forged relationships with a number of the biggest manufacturers, like Pillsbury, Dove, Betty Crocker, General Mills, Pedigree, and others, to offer their printable coupons on its site. The system is a breeze: click the "Clip" check box for the coupons you want, hit the "Print" button on the top right of the page, and you will automatically be prompted to register (or sign in if you are a member). After completing the registration you will be asked to download the coupon printer (a small software program that will stay on your computer, so you won't have to do this each time) and accept the terms and conditions.

Once you are done, the coupons will automatically be printed out from your computer's default printer.

Manufacturers' sites remain one of my favorite places because you can print coupons *and* get free promotional offers like refunds, freebies and coupons in one place. Most of the coupons on these sites are not found on any other site. For example, last time I checked, Betty Crocker had coupons for cookie mix, frosting, Warm Delights Minis, baking mix, Cheerios (multiple kinds), Cinnamon Chex, Cookie Crisp cereal, frozen boxed vegetables, frozen bagged vegetables, Progresso products, potato products, Chex Mix Bars, Chewy Granola Bars, Chex Mix, Cheerios Snack Mix, Fruit Gushers, Yoplait yogurt, and YoPlus all right on the website. These are some of my favorite manufacturers' sites for printable coupons and promotions:

- ❖ 3m.com
- ❖ BettyCrocker.com
- ❖ Colgate.com
- ❖ Gortons.com
- ❖ Hersheys.com
- ❖ Keebler.com
- ❖ Kelloggs.com
- ❖ Kraftfoods.com
- ❖ Langers.com
- ❖ Lysol.com
- ❖ PG.com
- ❖ RiteAid.com

One interesting feature some manufacturers' sites offer is a sign-up program for coupons by mail. I just received a booklet worth over $30 in coupons from ConAgra, which included Healthy Choice products, among others, and $5.50 in coupons from Dove.

There are some limitations with printable coupons, of course. Coupons.com's biggest problem, to me, is the selection. The last time I used the site, I found only 118 coupons available for my zip code, and more than half of those were for other retail outlets (e.g., Olan Mills Photos, ExtraSpacestorage.com and Shari's Berries) while, in contrast, my coupon-clipping service (Select Coupon Program) had nearly a thousand different selections. Manufacturers' sites offer a wider array for those particular manufacturers' products, but you have to surf multiple such sites to acquire a decent variety of coupons, which can be a bit time-consuming.

Each site requires the user to provide personal information, which some people are wary to do (although as we discussed before, this is a great way to get free home mailers!). Also, most printable coupon discounts only go as high as 35¢ or 70¢, which might not really help on those expensive products. Last, and most important, not all stores accept these coupons. At a recent Supershopping Spree I did in Philadelphia (where I bought $210 worth of groceries for $7), I found out that the Acme supermarket, one of the biggest chains in that area, did not accept most printable coupons. Thus, it is important that you check with your local stores to find out if they accept them. Food Lion and A&P now have coupons you can download from their web site to your frequent shopper card. A&P stopped accepting printable coupons but have devised this method to still help the consumer. Depending on how Web-savvy you are and how often you think you will use this alternative, this may become another criterion for selecting your supermarket.

My advice is to check the sites that offer your favorite products on a weekly basis. Try the manufacturers' sites of items you use regularly. You'll often be pleasantly surprised by the good deals, free downloadable recipe books, and rebates you'll find.

As Digital Coupons Online

In the last decade there has been a lot of hype about digital coupons, but the truth is that these types of coupons really have not taken off in any meaningful way.

Digital grocery coupons are nothing fancy. They are just coupons that can be uploaded to your store grocery card or mobile phone (although at this time most grocery stores do not use the mobile phone option). Unfortunately, the availability of digital coupons is extremely limited, mostly because consumers have not caught on enough to make them a truly viable option. Still, if you are interested in this alternative, take a look at Cellfire.com. Cellfire is an online system that allows you to simply and easily upload digital coupons directly to your store loyalty card (more discussion on store loyalty cards in chapter 4) or your mobile phone.

First, you'll enter your zip code to check which stores in your neighborhood use digital coupons. Then, you choose the coupons you want and you can save them to your grocery card or cell phone by simply following the online instructions. When you go to the store to shop, present your card at the checkout as usual and the savings will be automatically applied. The discount will appear on your receipt as "Cfire." (When you use coupons from your mobile phone, you just show your phone at the checkout to redeem.)

In the future, I expect more digital coupons to sprout up, but as I said, there has been hype about them for over fifteen years and nothing concrete has been established. So until something more significant is introduced, I would not recommend spending too much time on digital.

• • •

THE SIMPLEST WAY TO FILE

·········

Now that you have all those coupons, what are you going to do with them? One primary quality distinguishes the casual couponer, who is content with penny-ante savings, from the Supershopper, who goes for the highest dividends possible. That quality is a willingness to *organize*.

Now, don't back away in annoyance, saying you "can't do that." If you have ever planned a family meal or a day's chores or what your child is going to wear to school, then you have the organizational ability to understand and profit from my filing system.

Besides, it's the simplest system in the world. All it takes is one large envelope and a rubber band.

I know there are couponers who have developed more complicated systems for keeping track of their cash-offs. One person I knew in Ohio had a beautiful old wooden mail sorter in her kitchen, and she kept her coupons filed in the pigeonholes. Many people thumbtack their coupons to a bulletin board so they can see them easily, and others keep theirs tucked, in glorious disarray, behind cookie jars, in cookbooks, and scattered over counters. All of these methods, I guess, work all right for the people who use them. I prefer my one big accordion envelope.

I keep the envelope in a top drawer in my kitchen cabinet. In it I place all the coupons I currently have in stock, filed alphabetically according to the *type* of product they're for and then the brand name. For example, under the Household category I have in alpha order: All, Dawn, Downy, Era, Fab, Gain, and so on. I also include all my printable coupons in there, in the same categories. Your categories may be different from mine, depending on the size and nature of your family. But to give you an idea of my single-envelope system, here are the categories I prefer to use:

Batteries	Frankfurters	Peanuts, etc.
Breads	Frozen Foods	Pickles
Cakes	Household Items	Pizza
Candy	Ice Cream	Popcorn
Canned Goods	Juices	Rice/Pasta
Cheese	Lightbulbs	Snacks
Coffee	Noodles	Soda
Crackers/Cookies	Oil	Spices
Drug Items	Paper Goods	Tea

Some of these categories contain coupons for several different kinds of items. "Drug Items," for example, includes deodorants, toothpastes, and all kinds of "notions." "Household Items" contains cleansers, detergents, mop heads, and so on. And there must be a dozen kinds of fruits and vegetables in "Canned Goods" and "Frozen Foods." Practice has taught me where to look for what I need.

Behind the "Tea" coupons, under "Miscellaneous," I put all of my rain checks—the certificates that stores give you when they are out of an advertised special, so you can buy at the advertised price when the item is back in stock. After the rain checks I alphabetically group coupons for free samples, which, like cash-offs themselves, often come in specially marked packages. All told, I have about two to four hundred coupons in the envelope at one time—most of them cash-offs and some of them for free samples or products.

Needless to say, it's not a slender envelope. I keep it secure with a strong elastic band, and when I get new coupons (which is just about every day), I first put them under the band on the

outside of the envelope. Next, I file them in the appropriate category when I have an extra five minutes or so—about every week or ten days. It's the simplest filing system imaginable, and it takes almost no time at all.

One important point to remember about coupons: most cash-offs have an expiration date (ED) printed on them somewhere, and no matter how clear your filing is, if you let them sit in the envelope or drawer beyond that date, you're going to be out of luck. You'll often find that magazine and newspaper coupons are good "for 30 days" or "for 90 days." This means thirty or ninety days from the periodical's date of issue. Some couponers highlight the expiration dates with a yellow Magic Marker or simply circle them. This makes them easier to see, both for you and for the checker. Whenever I file new coupons, I keep an eye out for those EDs, and pull any coupons that are about to lapse, so I can try to fit them into my next shopping trip before they do. This is especially important at the end of the calendar year, since a great many coupons expire on December 31. But oftentimes if my couponed item is not on sale, I'll deliberately let the coupon expire and wait for the next coupon and sale. With over 300 billion coupons issued I know another coupon is just around the corner.

PREPARING FOR YOUR SHOPPING TRIP: STEP BY STEP

Great! In step 3 we have gathered our coupons and organized them in our file; in step 2 we chose our favorite store and back-ups; and, in step 1, we compiled our grocery list. There is just one more step before we hit the store: comparing our in-ad coupons, store flyers, and manufacturers' cash-offs to figure out where we want to shop this week and how we will go about getting the products we need. The key here, as I've said before, is flexibility and a willingness to give up the crazy obsession with brand or store loyalty.

When I'm about to go shopping, the first thing I do, like any good Supershopper, is to check the local sales. This helps me decide which store I am going to use this week, and believe me, that varies quite a lot. Most stores have the same volume of in-store sales, but the products they discount are offered in a cyclical pattern. Some "experts" advise you always to stick with one store since eventually the sales will come your way, but to me, this is a poor decision. For example, if you stick with one store and shop there once a week, you will be at its mercy in regard to which products you can get on sale. If you tackle a couple of nearby stores, you can hunt down the bargains and get what you need when you need it. While I wouldn't go very far out of my way for a few 10¢ or 15¢ coupons, if I'm armed with a batch of valuable 50¢ and $1 cash-offs, I consider traveling a must if I can track down a nearby store that's doubling or tripling coupons.

Doubling is a practice that is quite common in areas of intense competition. Sometimes this promotion is temporary, giving the store time to evaluate its success. Other times, as in my area, doubling has been going on for years. Each store determines the limit of the double coupon and may also set a limit as to the number of coupons doubled in a single shopping trip. What it means is that the store will give you *twice* the value of your coupons instead of the face value. Thus, a 50¢ coupon is actually worth $1, and a $1 coupon is worth $2. Store managers do this to entice you into using their store rather than their competitors', and the practice can be a real boon for the shopper. Occasionally, a store will even *triple* the face value of your coupons. This is rare, but it's a bonanza well worth hunting for. You can simply ask the manager at your local supermarket (or sometimes they will have the policies listed on their websites) to find out which of your stores double or triple.

Printable coupons, as I mentioned earlier, are becoming quite popular as well, and for many they form another criterion when preparing their weekly shopping trips. Again, you can find out which of your local stores accept printable coupons by asking or checking each store's website.

Every shopper will weigh each criterion differently. Say you are not terribly tech-savvy (like myself) and are not planning on using many printable coupons: you should focus on stores that double or triple and have frequent in-store sales. If none of your local stores double but there are some much farther away that do, you have to consider your travel expenses before making your choice.

After deciding which store can save me the most money, I get its weekly flyer and circle the specials that interest me. Then I go to my bulging envelope and thumb through it to see which coupons I can apply to which specials, and I pull them to take with me. Even though I have two hundred–plus coupons to look at, I'm pretty familiar with my file by now, and the check never takes more than five minutes (which is nothing, considering the savings it leads to).

Armed with the store's own in-ad coupons and a batch of manufacturers' cash-offs, I head for the supermarket.

Since I've done my planning beforehand, I meet few surprises when I get there. I may discover that orange juice shot up 60¢, but I'll have a Minute Maid coupon with me that will allow me to get three cartons of orange juice for the price the Normal Shopper is paying for two. Or I may find that ground chuck has just jumped to the price that sirloin was last week, but I'll be able to compensate for this by using a coupon for $1.25 off Oscar Mayer franks or by buying the featured meat of the week.

> There are very few products in the modern supermarket that you can't at least occasionally discount with coupons.

COUPON STRATEGIES

What can you use coupons for?

The answer is practically everything. There are very few products in the modern supermarket that you can't at least occasionally discount with coupons. Realizing substantial savings on your food bill, then, is only a matter of being sure you have the relevant cash-offs with you when you enter the store.

Using Coupons for "Off-Products"

Your most extensive savings are usually on household cleaning aids, health and beauty products, cereals, pet foods, packaged items, paper goods, canned goods, and processed foods. The makers of fresh meat and produce don't offer very many cash-offs, so I call them "off-products."

There are, however, ways to cut your meat and produce bills with coupons. For example, some companies that don't sell meat will give you coupons for meat because they want you to use their products *with* the meat. Borden periodically offers cash-offs for ground beef so you will use its cheese for cheeseburgers. These coupons can save you as much as $2.50 on a single purchase. Ragú does the same thing with its spaghetti sauces. Wishbone also issues coupons for produce. A few weeks ago I was sent $2 worth of coupons for the purchase of fresh vegetables or mushrooms, presumably so I would remember its name as I was mixing the salad to go with the dressing. Recently, I found a coupon for $1 off produce with the purchase of Kraft mayonnaise. When summer rolls around, and barbecues are in season, Kingsford charcoal has been known to pair up with Budweiser beer to offer $20 off meat or poultry. Between all of these great purchase opportunities, it's never too difficult to find deals on all of those "off-products."

Other coupons are issued as a kind of reward for buying a certain manufacturer's products. I remember a great deal where Johnson & Johnson gave out $7 in coupons to anyone who had bought *any* five of their products. The coupons were applicable against any grocery item; I used my $7 to buy enough salad greens for a week!

Another trend in the supermarket is branded produce, milk, and eggs. I've been getting coupons on Smart Balance, Silk, and

Simply Smart Milk. Eggland, Land o' Lakes, and Disney are now branding eggs. And Foxy, Del Monte, Green Giant, and Dole have pineapple, lettuce, celery, and carrots all boasting brand names and all heavily couponed. My last purchase of half a gallon of Smart Balance Milk was $.99 after a manufacturer's coupon and the store sale.

I mention these examples to show you that you can even save money with coupons on nonprocessed foods.

Buying in Bulk

Another savings trick is to buy in large quantities, taking advantage of both coupons and sales. If Del Monte canned vegetables are on sale ten cans for $2, I may buy ten cans and get no more for three weeks.

An even more dramatic example is the bulk purchase I made of toothpaste a while back. When Colgate introduced its then-new Total toothpaste, it advertised it at $1.89 a tube. Sensing a bargain, I decided to stock up. In my coupon envelope I found a half dozen $1 off Colgate coupons, and from friends I gathered four more. Then I went to the store and bought ten tubes; at 89¢ each with the coupons, my total outlay was $8.90.

Sound extravagant? Not when you consider that a week later the normal price went into effect, and the price turned out to be $2.89 a tube. If I had bought those ten one at a time without my coupons, they would have cost me $28.90. So not only was I able to forget about shopping for toothpaste for months, but I ended up saving $20 besides. And this is not a rare type of bargain. This kind of thing happens all the time; you just need to keep your eyes peeled!

. . .

TECHNOLOGIES IN THE 21ST CENTURY

·········

New technologies have improved our lives in so many ways, and the Supershopping system is no exception—we use technology and the Internet to help us reach our goal, which is to save money and time. The hard part is figuring out which technologies can actually do this. I will do my best to provide unbiased reviews and feedback for each site, but since technologies change over time, be sure to visit one of my websites—SelectCouponProgram.com, CouponQueen.com, or RefundleBundle.com—for more up-to-date information.

Before we jump into the different types of technologies that are out there, it is important for you to understand where you fit in to the puzzle. I think there are three distinct groups that apply: those who are tech-savvy, those who are not, and those who are somewhere in the middle.

Me, I fall someplace in the middle. I don't know as much as my children do, but I am comfortable using my computer to do word processing, search the Internet, e-mail friends, and a little more. I did need a bit of help to test some of the things I am going to discuss in this chapter. A few of my children's friends have the iPhone and love it, but they had to show me how to use it.

I don't claim to be a technology expert, but I am an expert in saving at the checkout, so I know what will work and what will not.

Also, just because I may recommend a certain tool, don't feel obligated to use it. Do what you feel comfortable with and don't be afraid to ask someone for help.

Okay; with that disclaimer out of the way, let's get started.

· · ·

Finding the Best Websites

First off, don't be fooled by the thousands of websites out there claiming that they can save you money. Today's technology has made it easy enough for anyone to create and launch a website. This is why it is so important to take a careful look at the credibility behind the information you find. Everyone has different ideas on the best ways to save. Some people tell you to buy generic, or store-brand, products, others tell you to stick with national brands. Who is right?

The answer lies in their credibility. Ask yourself the following questions about the source: Have you ever heard of the person giving the advice? Have they been featured on TV or in print? How is the quality of their website? Do they offer a privacy policy on their site? Do they only focus on supermarket savings? The answers to these questions will let you know whether or not to trust the advice they are giving. Always read the fine print and follow your gut.

THESE ARE SOME OF MY FAVORITE SITES:

My Sites:

1. CouponQueen.com
2. RefundleBundle.com
3. SelectCouponProgram.com

My Top Three:

1. Coupons.com—the #1 site for printable coupons
2. Upromise.com—a 529k college savings program tied into your frequent shopping cards; register all your cards, and each time you shop, the savings will automatically be added to your account. Then transfer your accumulated funds to a 529.

3. SmartSource.com—great site with free grocery sale finder (no registration required)

Other Notable Sites

❖ Amazon.com
❖ Cellfire.com
❖ FreshDirect.com
❖ Peapod.com
❖ P&GeSaver.com
❖ RedPlum.com
❖ Shortcuts.com

Other Types of Savings Sites (look for the promotions, special offers, coupons, or rebates links)

❖ AceHardware.com
❖ Bing.com/cashback
❖ CoolSavings.com
❖ DailyCandy.com
❖ DealCatcher.com
❖ MyPoints.com—ability to transfer mileage between carriers
❖ MySavings.com
❖ OfficeDepot.com
❖ Restaurant.com—discounts on restaurants, always wait for the 70 or 80% sale
❖ RetailMeNot.com
❖ RiteAid.com
❖ RitzCamera.com
❖ ShopAtHome.com
❖ Staples.com
❖ TrueValueHardware.com

• • •

Checking Sales Online @ CouponQueen.com

Checking store flyers is time-consuming. I know because for the last thirty years I have been checking them every week. With the help of my tech-savvy children and with a lot of hard work, I have created a system on my website that allows people to search their local supermarket circulars without leaving the comfort of their computer chair.

The system is fun, easy, and designed to mimic my shopping list preparation, and it doesn't require much knowledge of the Internet. (Look at me! I'm not exactly your most technically savvy person, and I can do it!) Enter your zip code, as directed on the site, choose your favorite store and you will see a list of all the items for sale. From there you can save the items to your CouponQueen.com grocery list, add other items that might not be on sale (but that you need anyway) or even limit your search to your favorite brands or products by entering in a keyword. Since you can switch from store to store with the click of the mouse, you can compare store sales in seconds. You can add or remove favorites and update your online shopping list as often as necessary.

This service is completely free and syncs with your iPhone if you have one. I encourage you to try it.

Using Smartphone Applications

Smartphone applications are already making their way into mainstream shopping. I expect that there will be more of these applications in the future, but since a large majority of people who use coupons do not have smartphones, it is not common-place quite yet.

Some people I speak with are confused as to what constitutes a smartphone. While there is no standard definition, the term typically refers to any cell phone with computer capabilities. Some examples are Apple's iPhone, Motorola's Q, HP's iPAQ, RIM's BlackBerry, and Palm's Treo.

The most well-known smartphone grocery shopping application is Grocery iQ; Coupons, Inc. (Coupons.com) recently purchased the company that developed it. Grocery iQ is a grocery list that you can create and edit on your iPhone or a phone that uses the Android platform, but what makes it so useful is its database of almost every product at your local grocery store. It's beneficial because you can add not just the category of item, but the exact brand you prefer, so not just mustard but Gulden's mustard.

A new functionality will allow you to download coupons to your store loyalty card from the iPhone, which can be used at the checkout. Recently, I borrowed an iPhone from one of my son's friends to test this application. I started by creating the same shopping list I have on Microsoft Word. When I got to the store I was able to locate all of the products on my list. The application was correct that the store did indeed carry the items in question. I liked how the system organized the items by aisle, the same way I organize my list. I could also add items to my favorites list for later, and track my previous shopping history. If you keep a favorites list, that list stays intact for each and every shopping trip. There's no need to redo the entire list.

However, I was unable to find out which items were on sale using the application. I also found it a little hard to match my coupons with the items since I couldn't see the entire list on one page.

Overall, I thought the application was cute, but not really for me. However, I wouldn't be surprised if the application was changed and updated soon. Now that Coupons, Inc., owns the application, I expect the company will find a way to match printable coupons with the items on my list.

The one thing that the programs I tested seemed to lack was a focus on savings so I set out to create an application that shops like I do called: The Coupon Queen iPhone application. For the first time ever, I have consolidated thousands of grocery fliers into one central and easy-to-use application.

This application locates your position using the GPS in the phone and finds and sorts most of the grocery stores in your area (by closest distance to you). Choose your favorite store and search by either grocery category, like dairy, meat, produce, frozen, etc., or see an entire list of what is on sale in the store. Last, add the items to your online grocery list for use when you visit the store.

Since I know I don't like to spend a lot of time on my phone, I created the application to sync with my CouponQueen.com website. This way you can go online, create your list, and with the click of a button send your list directly to your iPhone.

STEP 3:
USE COUPON POWER
·········

Coupon Power is key to the Supershopping system, as it brings in the shoppers' most valuable asset. Here are the major points of step 3:

1. Find coupons.

You can find coupons on specially marked packages, in newspapers and magazines, in home mailers, through my very own Select Coupon Program Site, and from the Internet (both with digital and printable coupons). Trading with friends and family will increase your supply.

2. Keep a consistent filing system.

To profit from coupons, you have to be able to find them easily. One simple filing method is to keep your coupons arranged alphabetically, divided by category, in a single large envelope.

3. Don't be timid!

Contrary to popular opinion, most store personnel are *not* offended by the heavy coupon user. Heavy couponing means good sales for the store, plus healthy handling fees. So you need not be embarrassed about using your Coupon Power: it benefits the store as well as the shopper.

4. Shop national brands.

Only the big national companies can afford to issue coupons. Therefore, Coupon Power means buying the national brand names almost exclusively, even though the generic, or store, brands appear cheaper at first glance.

5. Don't forget about expiration dates.

Clipping cents-off coupons can save you up to 65% on your grocery bill every week, but only if you use them wisely and regularly. Letting them lie in a drawer until they expire won't save you a penny. It will help if you organize your coupon file with the nearest expiration dates at the front in each category.

6. Be on the lookout for doubling.

Stores in stiff competition offer double value for coupons as a means of inducing you to buy. It's definitely worthwhile hunting around for a store that's doubling, even if it's not your "favorite" store. Doubling can mean significant extra savings.

7. Watch for online sales and useful smart-phone applications.

Online store sales go further than the weekly print flyer. Check your store's promotion tab for additional savings opportunities. In addition, there are hundreds of websites out there with special programs and promotional deals, as well as smartphone applications and digital coupon systems.

8. Create an online shopping list.

Keeping your shopping list online allows you to update and change it without creating an entirely new list each week. Plus, it makes it easier to find items on sale when you are updating an old list. You can do this on our website CouponQueen.com and/ or create a Microsoft document.

And that's Coupon Power! Now that we have what I call our "ammunition," we're finally going to enter the store! Come with me—I'll guide you!

STEP 4:

Shop Smart

···

Walking the Walk

HERE WE ARE: that scary leviathan known as the Supermarket! The very word "supermarket" might sound intimidating to some. It's not just a market; it is a *super* market. The sheer size and extensive product selection can be overwhelming. To conquer the *super*market, you need to be a *Super*shopper. It can be hard to know how to navigate the ins and outs of your local grocery store, but with the proper plan, you can master the market and make it work for you.

In this chapter I will not only discuss store layout and provide some helpful shopping tips, but I'll also bring you into the store with me, the Coupon Queen, as your virtual guide as I navigate the store for super savings! At the end of the chapter, we'll talk about how you can use the stores' own rewards programs to further your saving potential. We'll end at the checkout with a shopping cart full of supplies and a grand total that you won't believe!

· · ·

HOW *NOT* TO SHOP

· · · · · · · · ·

If you've ever watched the way most shoppers scurry up and down the supermarket aisles, snatching and plucking with barely a glance at the products they're acquiring, you might well agree with me that the "careful shopper" is probably the figment of some hopeful consumerist's imagination: a hypothetical being that has yet to make an appearance on this planet.

Sure, there are always a few odd ducks blocking traffic to look at labels and compare prices, but if you watch them closely you'll notice that somewhere along the line—usually between the Pringles display and the end-of-aisle special on canned peaches—even these rare birds pick up a couple of obvious "impulse buys." (Come on, did you really *plan* on buying two boxes of Mallomars?) In fact, according to Scarborough Research, only 14% of us stick to our shopping lists completely, while 86% regularly fall off course and buy things on impulse! Think of the extra money being spent!

Most of us are used to walking into the supermarket pretty much unprepared. We may have a mental list, but you know how easily we can be distracted by the "limited edition" Edy's ice cream and forget all about the nonfat yogurt we meant to buy. Lacking prior preparation, the Normal Shopper has no recourse but to buy from memory and on impulse. That impulse may take thirty seconds or it may take three, but unless the shopper has a phenomenal memory, the decisions he makes in the aisle will bear only a sketchy relation to the gaps on his shelves at home.

Sure, most of us rush through the store, not wanting to spend hours grocery shopping. But you *can* shop successfully for a family in thirty minutes. I've done it many times. It just takes some prior preparation if you're not going to get stuck with thirteen bottles of on-sale soda and no main course. Remember, as we've discussed, the more time you spend shopping, the more money you'll spend. That's a given.

Impulse buying is not really the fault of the consumer. As we saw in step 2, the supermarket has an unlimited supply of strategies up its sleeve to get you to buy things you never thought you needed, and without the proper know-how, how can an average American stand up against multinational corporations and experienced market-research teams whose sole goal is to get you to spend your hard-earned cash?

We've discussed the first answer already: being aware of the traps and avoiding them at all costs. But we're human, and it's hard. Thus, we can double our chances of shopping smart if we learn how to maneuver efficiently through the store, following a planned course to get us in and out without unnecessary meandering through the endless aisles and colorful displays used to capture our attention (and our money).

MARKETING TECHNIQUES TO RECOGNIZE

First of all, there are *displays*. In any one week, your local market will very likely be featuring sales, specials, and display presentations of dozens of old and new items. A new soap powder will lure you with an "introductory" or "get-acquainted" offer, while an old one next to it displays a proud "75¢ off" tag. At the end of one aisle a pyramid of tuna fish cans beckons you with a giant "special" sign, while around the corner tomatoes are offered, prepacked, at "5 for $1."

The important thing to remember about all these inducements to buy is that a *"sale" is not always a sale*.

There are, of course, bona fide sales going on all the time, but the Normal Shopper seldom distinguishes between these and the flashy nonsales. One good way to determine which is which is to check your local paper for advertised sales. By sticking with these, you can be sure your bargain is actually a bargain. One common example, which we will delve into in more detail later, is the package "deals" many stores advertise as sales. A retailer will "bundle" several packages of a product and label the full set as a "sale" when, in fact, the grouping costs the exact same as buying that number of the products individually. Simple math will prove this to be true, so take a moment to crunch the numbers if you think you might be witness to a false sale such as this.

Supermarket *design* is another tool market managers use to get us to buy products we might not necessarily have on our list. Although markets are ostensibly laid out along the lines of shopping convenience, what the manager considers when he is deciding to put the rutabagas next to the cheese dip or at the end of the soda aisle is an elementary salesman's question: "How can I get my customers to see the greatest number of products in the shortest period of time?"

With thousands of new items coming onto the shelves every year, store owners obviously can't expect their customers to see everything. So they try for the next best thing. They arrange the stores so the shopper must at least pass through every section before leaving. The reason the dairy department is so often at the rear of the store, for example, is because it has what market people call "drawing power." It acts as a magnet because practically everyone needs to buy milk and eggs; as you head for this department, you pass numerous other items on the way.

High-profit items, moreover, are often placed in the first aisle, which you "hit" when you still feel financially flush, or near the registers, where you are a captive audience. Produce, for example, is both a high-profit and a high-impulse item. It's no accident that it's often placed in aisle 1. Nor is it accidental that candy and gum are stocked at the checkout counter, where they will be all but irresistible to a shopper waiting in line with a whining child.

Pricing, too, is worked out to make you think you are getting bargains even when you are not. Because the market experts have discovered that odd-cent prices are somehow mystically more attractive to shoppers than even-cent prices, you'll seldom find a can of vegetables going for $1.28 or $1.30; it's usually the magical $1.29. To the Normal Shopper, presumably, that translates as a bargain, whereas $1.30 would be somehow suspect.

The same goes for the reason why products are never a solid "$4.00," but rather "$3.99." Our brains always process the first number of a series initially, and it takes us a bit longer to take the later digits into account. Thus, our eyes are actually "seeing" the "3" before the "99" and tricking our brains into thinking that this is a much lower price than a simple "$4.00."

By using all these techniques the supermarkets are playing the game the way they know best, and it's no secret that when we buy more, they profit. I like to look at all these techniques not as inescapable traps but as opportunities for gaining a greater awareness of what skills you need in order to be a Supershopper. Skills as simple as having a distinguishing eye and understanding marketing tricks and techniques can go a long way in those long aisles. I also find that over time, Supershopping has helped me hone my basic math skills, as I am constantly doing quick calculations in my head in order to determine whether or not "sales" I encounter in the store are truly the bargains they appear to be.

Above all, I hope hearing something about these common

techniques will put you on your guard, even make you a little suspicious the next time you enter a supermarket. With a little observation, you will see how the supermarkets, in the honest pursuit of profits, manipulate their customers' responses, and how, by becoming aware of that manipulation, you can turn it to your own advantage. Let's see how.

UNDERSTANDING THE SUPERMARKET LAYOUT

Most supermarkets are designed in roughly the same way. Dairy products are on the outside along with meats and fresh produce. Essentials like bread are almost always at the back of the store, ensuring that you must walk through the entire market to get to what you want. The middle aisles, where most consumers spend the majority of their time, are actually the least useful in terms of practical products: junk food, snacks, and sodas are found here.

I find that "perimeter shopping" nets me the best savings, whereby I simply walk around the outer perimeter of the store, since most of the essentials are found there, and at much lower prices. However, we cannot simply ignore the interior aisles. You need to understand how best to navigate through the trenches of the supermarket, and I have several helpful tips, along with the sample store layout on the next page. You can use this as a reference as we go on our "tour." Of course, every store is laid out with subtle differences, but this map (and the tips that follow) will give you an idea of the pattern many stores follow. Knowing where "your" items generally are in any store will make you a smarter shopper: first because of the time saved, and also because price comparisons, and sales, will help determine the best purchase.

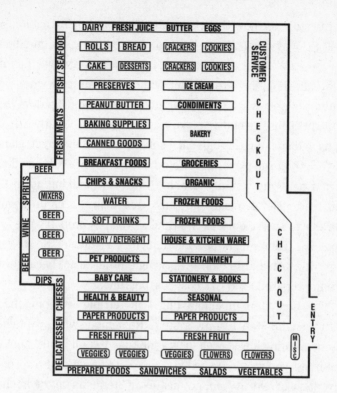

Some people find it helps to create a rough hand-drawn or computer-generated map of the stores they frequent. Many stores even have their layouts online. I, for one, am so familiar with my store that I have a mental picture of how it is laid out, so I find a formal printed map unnecessary. What is vital, however, is being familiar enough with your store (or stores) that you can anticipate what route you will want to take. Once you pick that route, stick with it so you do not get distracted! There will be times, naturally, when you will need to veer off your standard path for certain items (items you may not need on a regular basis), and that is *fine*, assuming you get yourself back on track without spending too much time in these other sections!

Like I said before, few of us really consider the path we follow in the store, or how that path will affect our buying habits. We just go. Why do shoppers tend to dive right into the middle of the store? Well, for the most part, it's because very few of us are strategic shoppers. We wander without a plan, and when you enter a store, what does your impulse tell you to do? Walk straight! Thus, we end up picking a random aisle directly in front of us and snaking through each subsequent aisle, maybe glancing briefly at the placard over our heads, maybe not. If you don't own a pet, why would you waste your time walking down the pet food aisle? It makes no sense, but many of us do it, and here's why: we're curious. We think, "Well, it's probably not *just* dog food. There might be something here I can use!" So we venture down this aisle, and every single other aisle, because we are unprepared. And this costs us, big time.

The first step in eliminating this terrible shopping habit returns us to step 1 of my system. Remember when we talked about creating a list? Well, now's the time to pull it out! Look at the items you said you needed—and don't forget to do a proper inventory of *everything*, not just food! Step outside the kitchen for a minute. Check your bathroom for toiletry items, your laundry room for things like fabric softener and detergent, and any other parts of your house where you store grocery items. It sometimes helps to arrange your shopping list in the same order you will hit the different sections of the store. For example, if the first thing you'll see when you enter your store is the produce section, and produce is on your shopping list, you should put the items in that category at the *top*. That way, you don't waste time scanning your list back and forth trying to figure out what you have purchased and what you have not. Remember: the more time you waste in the store, the higher the risk of spending more than you planned on! Just keep in mind that every store is laid out a bit differently, so don't drive yourself too crazy with this.

We picked our store in step 2, so look back over the store sale flyers and in-ad coupons as we discussed in step 3. Compare those flyers to your coupon file and make notes on which items you will be saving on. With this degree of organization and preparation, you'll strongly reduce the odds that you will veer from your list. Of course, you have to be willing to alter course in case a sale is no longer valid or if you find something better when you arrive.

WALKING DOWN THE AISLE

Since you've divided your list into categories based on the aisles in the store, we can now check out your list and go to the first aisle on whichever side of the store matches your list.

So we're in our first aisle. What do we see first? Assuming we're coming from the entrance of the store and heading toward the back, the first items we see will generally not be essentials. The middle of the aisle is where the products you want will most likely be, since the store manager wants you to walk through the entire aisle instead of just grazing the edges. When shoppers target their item in a certain aisle, grab it, and do an about-face back to where they came from, marketing specialists call that the "boomerang effect." Supermarket managers want to encourage us—dare I say, force us—to go through the entire aisle. They want to maximize the number of products we see during this journey, so they put the major brand names in the center of the aisle itself.

In general, supermarkets try to group like products together; for example, they may put mustard in a display next to the case where the hot dogs are to get you to buy in combination. However, you'll notice that there is also mustard available in the

> **Supermarket managers want to encourage us—dare I say, force us—to go through the entire aisle.**

condiment aisle, but for a much lower price. Why? Again, it's about impulse buys. The supermarket hopes that when you grab your hot dogs, you'll think, "Oh! What a coincidence! My favorite mustard is right here and what's a hot dog without mustard?" By knowing this supermarket secret, you will remind yourself to check the specific product aisle to see if the prices are cheaper there. Nine times out of ten, they will be.

Another common retailing ploy takes place in the frozen food section. What are the first things you see when you enter the aisle from the front? Probably ice cream, frozen pops, and other delicious, tempting snacks. Common items like frozen vegetables are stuck all the way in the back, so we have to go past everything else to get to them. The trick is to walk quickly through the heads of the aisles to target the products you actually *need*, or to come around from the back of the aisle. We all need vegetables. We probably don't have six pints of Ben & Jerry's ice cream very high on our list.

Train Your Eyes

Knowing where to look is the most important part of alert shopping. There is a real science to product placement in grocery stores, and the manufacturers with the most money and the best-selling products always get the sweet spots. As a rule, retailers will generally put these premium items at eye level to get your attention, so always be sure to scan above and below where your eyes naturally want to look in order to find the best bargains. This is not to say that the eye-level products won't net you good bargains at times, but it is foolish not to look elsewhere as well. As always, refer to your list and your coupon file or store flyer to see which products and brands will give you the best deals.

Have kids? It might be best to leave them at home for your weekly shopping trips, as retailers specifically target young children in regard to where they put their products. Things like sugary (and expensive) cereals and candies are always placed much lower—why, you might ask, would they do that if they want me to buy it? The answer is obvious! It's not *your* eyes they want to capture, but your kids'! And when your child is crying and pleading for you to buy his or her favorite brand of cookies, it is so easy to give in to avoid a full-blown tantrum.

Okay, now here's a test: Let's say you see a package of Hefty one-zip bags for $2.39 right in front of you when you first glance at the shelf. You then glance three shelves above it, a bit higher than your head, and notice a private-label brand running at $1.89. Which do you choose? Be careful now. We pull up the flyer, and Hefty does not happen to be on sale today. We knew this going in, but we did bring along a manufacturer's coupon for buy-one-get-half-off-the-second. So you have two choices: buy one package of the generic brand for $1.89, or buy *two* boxes of Hefty for $2.39, or $1.20 per package. You will spend more money opting for the latter choice, but you'd get a better deal. Do you have a family? If so, you probably could use the extra box, and you'll be saving in the long run. Plastic bags never go bad, and perhaps at some point down the line you will be able to redeem the proof of purchase seals on the Hefty boxes for a cash refund, a bonus generally only brand-name manufacturers offer. We will dive into the world of refunding in the next chapter, but suffice it to say, it makes more sense to get the extra package and to stick with the national brand.

Don't Follow Your Nose!

Scent is used all the time by store managers to entice you to go where they want you to go. I don't recommend heading into the store with a clothespin on your nostrils, but it is important that you be aware of the subliminal mind games the store is playing to lure you around by the nose. Be conscious of where you are going and you will be less likely to stray from your target and buy extra items.

The obvious smell tactic is free samples. These little stands are both nose-grabbing and eye-catching, because after all, who doesn't like free food? And it's not so much that the samples are there to make you buy *that* specific product. Oh no, that would be far too simple. They are simply bringing you to that area and getting your mind in the mood for that type of food so that you will be more likely to buy an expensive product in that vicinity. For example, a store manager might decide to place a sample of chicken teriyaki from the frozen entrée section next to the barbecue sauces and spice section. You might be tempted to go back to the frozen food aisle, but you do have boneless chicken breasts in your freezer at home, so maybe instead you will impulsively pick up a bottle of teriyaki sauce for later in the week.

Ever wonder why the fresh-baked bread section is always in the back? Think about it: that aroma is a lure. By going all the way to the back of the store to see what smells so good, you are again forced to walk through the entire store *twice*—once on your way there, and again on your way back. See a pattern here? The grocery store is appealing to each of your senses to give you an appetite for eating, thereby increasing the chances you will overbuy. Here's a tip: never go to the grocery store hungry!

> **Here's a tip: never go to the grocery store hungry!**

Be Suspicious of Supposed Deals

A lot of times, a deal isn't really a deal. Sound odd? It's not when you consider that store retailers will often try to market something as a bargain when, in reality, it isn't the best deal you can find. Merely seeing a sale sign on something is likely to cost us money. In fact, consumers will statistically buy 30% to 100% more than they otherwise might have if an item is advertised as a bargain, according to a survey conducted by Inmar, a coupon-processing agent.

Be wary of flashy advertisements selling things like "10 for $10!" Not that this isn't a great deal, but many times you don't actually have to buy ten items to get the deal. Sometimes, you can buy just five items and still get them for $5. Be sure to read the fine print before assuming you have to pick up a whole batch of items you don't really need. Stocking up is a good idea, but only when you (1) truly need the item and (2) know you will use it before it spoils.

"Bundling," or, more properly, "multiple-unit pricing," is another technique designed to convince the unwary that they're getting away cheaply when they're not. Whenever you see a "two-for" or "five-for" sign, be on guard. Again, the implication of "sale" is very strong, but if you check the prices of three single cans of beans against the "three-for" price, you'll very often find that the package deal is no savings. Store owners price items as triplets and twins because they haven't been able to move them singly or they simply want to increase sales.

Bulk pricing can add to your savings if you read the rules carefully. My local Waldbaum's has been offering products for 88¢ but you must buy in multiples of ten. There may be 10 or 20 products included in the promotion but you have to buy in multiples of ten. So you can buy four salad dressings, two cans of cranberry sauce, two boxes of hot cocoa, two boxes of dryer sheets, five jars of gravy, three boxes of tea, and two boxes of stuffing— and get each item for 88¢. But let's say there are only three jars of gravy left on the shelf: you'll have to get two other participating products or else you'll be charged full price on everything.

A&P recently offered four twelve-packs of Pepsi and two bags of Frito-Lay snacks for $11. But you had to buy all six items in a single shopping trip for the special deal.

The key: read the sale requirements carefully.

Look Beyond End-of-Aisle Displays

I do love end-of-aisle displays. Most of them feature the weekly sale items—the items you find inside the flyer and hope to add to your shopping list without searching the entire store. But this is not always the case.

These, like the "end cap" displays clustered near them, are not always what they appear to be.

This has been a trick of the trade for decades now, and people *still* get suckered into it. When you reach the end of the aisle, you will often see a pyramid of products lined up, with a huge sign offering a "great bargain" like "Buy at the low low price of $1.89!!" Oftentimes the items displayed here are those the retailer is trying to get rid of because they just haven't been selling very well, and the price, in fact, is not the lowest you can come up with. Or they are high-profit items—things like crackers, lightbulbs, and beer—that the management understandably wants to move quickly. The implication of "bargain" is there, even when the items displayed are being sold at the normal price. Look in the center of the aisle, where the products are all lined up together, and see whether or not the end-of-aisle display is offering a sincerely low price or if it's just low compared to the higher-priced items of the same type. Recently Barilla pasta was featured on the end cap as "3 boxes for $5." On the aisle shelf I found Ronzoni for 99¢ a box. I quickly switched my purchase. After all, a deal is a deal.

So check the prices and the signs. Unless the display actually identifies itself as a sale display, the "feature of the week" may just be last week's "dud of the week."

> **Unless the display actually identifies itself as a sale display, the "feature of the week" may just be last week's "dud of the week."**

Stay Wise to Shelf Shuffling

A particularly sneaky trick, in my humble opinion, is that of "shelf shuffling." This is a common practice most supermarket chains employ, whereby the store managers regularly move items around in the store so shoppers have to walk around longer to find what they are looking for. This again leaves us vulnerable to impulse buys and entices us to buy more than we need.

The tactic is mostly used to get consumers to try new or less successful products. Thus, managers will move these products to the places where premium or top-selling items are normally found, like brand-name peanut butter. When shoppers go hunting for their favorite peanut butter, they instead find something completely different, or at least a different brand of the same product type. It's worth it to take a look at the new product, and compare its price to the one you normally buy. Who knows? You might just have a coupon for it that particular day! But don't be lured into buying something you don't need or is more expensive just because it is there.

A FEW HELPFUL HINTS

I thought I'd share with you some shopping tips that don't necessarily help you with saving, but will definitely make your experience more enjoyable and convenient.

If an item that was on sale in the store circular is out of stock when you get there, always get a rain check. This is a guarantee that you will be able to purchase the products at the sale price when it is back in stock. Many stores will allow you to get multiple rain checks in one shopping trip, so ask for as many as you need at the courtesy desk. Snapple 12-pack was just on sale for 2/$10. My family loves both the diet and regular. I asked for two rain checks, one for diet and one for regular. I was rewarded with both. Always ask. The worst they can do is say no! A rain check is a hedge against inflation. Even if the price doubles, you're guaranteed the sale price. Keep your rain checks for a future shopping trip (mine are in my miscellaneous category), and hand them over to the checker before she rings up your order. And who knows? Perhaps by the time the item is back in stock you'll have a good high-value coupon to use. A sample rain check is shown on the next page.

Shop at off times, like dinnertime (or afterward), to avoid crowds. Between the hours of 9:00 p.m. and 8:00 a.m., only 4%

RAINCHECK

STOP & SHOP

We are sorry, this item is not available.

Item _Celeste pizza for one cheese_ ☑ With The Card
Quantity _6_   Size _5.5oz_   PLU# _60164_
Store _532_   Dept. _Frozen_
Sale Price _2 for 1.00_   ☐ Regular
Signature _[signature]_   Date of Issue _11/03/09_

─────Cashier Use Only─────

Price at time of purchase_____

Form #73-1609 Rev. 6/97   Expires 30 days from date of issue.

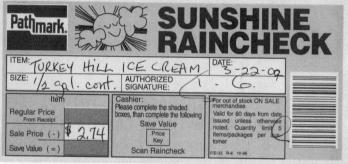

Pathmark SUNSHINE RAINCHECK

ITEM: _TURKEY HILL ICE CREAM_   DATE: _3-22-09_
SIZE: _1/2 gal. cont._   AUTHORIZED SIGNATURE: _1 - 6_

Item	Cashier: Please complete the shaded boxes, than complete the following Save Value	For out of stock ON SALE merchandise.
Regular Price From Receipt		Valid for 60 days from date issued unless otherwise noted. Quantity limit 5 items/packages per customer
Sale Price (-) $ 2.74	Price Key	
Save Value (=)	Scan Raincheck	F/E-33 R-6 10-96

CVS RAINCHECK

Store # _5454_   Date _5/31/09_
Item _Duracell AAA_
Size _8 pk_
Quantity _4_
Regular Price _____
SALE PRICE _$ 4.29_
Issued By _ERIC_

CASHIER USE
Purchased _____

OFFICE USE
Difference_____
Total Markdown Extension _____

Rev. 2/94 Item # 451435

MEAT SEAFOOD DELI BAKERY   FoodBasics

_723-9383_
the great atlantic & pacific tea co. inc.
Frozen
Item _Empire Turkey_
Whole Turkey _.99 lb_
Quantity _4_   Price
A & P Scearsdale _8/29/09_
(914) 723-9383
Authorized Signature _____ Date
EXP. 60 DAYS

of shoppers are hitting the stores, says the Coupon Council, so go late to have the place all to yourself! Oh, and statistically, the least crowded day of the week is Wednesday.

And know that the freshest products are always in the back. Don't be shy about reaching through past the older stuff to the back. I always do this with dairy and frozen foods. Check the dates before adding the cottage cheese and the like to your cart.

When you're going up and down the aisles, it's a good idea to separate, in the cart, items you have coupons for from those you don't. And be sure to tell the checkout clerk, before he or she starts ringing things up, that you're going to be using coupons or rain checks. This simplifies things, and, in fact, some stores even ask you to give them your coupons before the tallying begins.

SUPERSHOPPING:
A VIRTUAL TOUR WITH THE COUPON QUEEN!
·········

There are a lot of books out there that talk about couponing and saving at the supermarket. Indeed, I have written several books on the subject myself (this is my fourth), and even after almost four decades of teaching Supershopping to others, I am often asked: "Well, that's great, but how does it work?" Most books in this category are random smatterings of tips and suggestions for what to do when you enter a grocery store, but mine is the first to offer a step-by-step "tour" to make it very clear exactly how it's done.

As I enter the supermarket, I know I'm going to find a wealth of savings. I love the specially marked package deals in the cereal, snack, pet, household, and health and beauty aid aisles. I scour the blinking light coupon dispensers and look for tear-off coupons, refunds, and savings throughout the store. On a recent shopping trip, the reporter from the *Miami Herald* who accompanied me said she was sure I had radar to find these deals. So here are my secrets via our virtual tour.

My list is done and my coupons are set aside as I enter through the automatic doors. I take my coupon organizer with me, knowing that although I have carefully prepared my list, I will find a dozen or more unadvertised discounts that I can combine with my coupons. I leave the perimeter of the supermarket for last so the fresh produce, dairy, and meat will stay fresh before my checkout and journey home.

I head down the first aisle, featuring condiments, and spot a blinking light: a $1 French's mustard coupon. The mustard is on sale for $1.17. For 17¢ each I buy two—after all, it *is* cookout season. This is an example of an item perhaps not on our original list, but my family loves mustard and the deal is too good to pass up. Plus, mustard won't go bad! Kraft barbecue sauce is on my list and it's on sale this week for 75¢. My coupon reads "save $1 on two." For 50¢ I have two of my son Mark's favorite flavor: honey.

I round the corner to pet food and, lo and behold, Pup-Peroni, the treats that Zoya (my son Stuart's darling toy Yorkshire terrier) eats, are bundled in a buy-one-get-one-free (BOGOF) offer for $3.99. I save an extra $1 with a manufacturer's coupon. Total: $2.99 for two.

I hit one of my favorite aisles: cereal. I *never* pay full price here. This is one of the heaviest couponed sections in the store, and there are always cereals on sale. Today Kellogg's has a special: purchase four boxes for $6. I read about this sale in the circular and knew I was going to be buying four boxes, so I have four $1 off Kellogg's cereal coupons ready. My final cost is 50¢ per box, or $2 for all four boxes. And as a bonus, Kellogg's is offering a free T-shirt as a mail-in rebate! I'm already smiles from ear to ear.

Health and beauty aids can be very expensive, but not when you plan and dig out all those freebies, coupons, and refunds. I planned on buying Right Guard deodorant, which offered two for the price of one ($3.99). But my eyes drop down a shelf and I find a full purchase price refund on Sure, meaning I will get my money back in full (less the cost of my postage stamp). I change my purchase to the Sure. Brand flexibility here is the name of the game.

Detergents and household cleaners can almost bankrupt a shopper. But we coupon shoppers never have to fear. These

> **Brand flexibility here is the name of the game.**

cleaning products and paper goods can keep a long time. When I see the special offer to buy one, get two free, on Dynamo's and Fab's fifty-ounce bottles, I'm off and running. One bottle costs $6.99, minus an extra $1 with my manufacturer's coupon, and I get two for free. Because I have three $1 off coupons, I put nine bottles in my cart and end up getting all nine for just $18, or $2 per bottle. And that will last me a *long* time.

Next, on to dairy. I enjoy yogurt, and I keep the coupons for several brands, including Dannon, Yoplait, and Breyers. I am aware that Dannon yogurt, usually 99¢ a container, is on sale for 40¢ each. I use a $.40/4 coupon to further reduce my cost to 30¢ per container for the four that I need: a savings of 69¢ each, or $2.76.

Produce comes next. Because some produce and fruit are now branded, I have coupons for Fresh Express packaged lettuce, Del Monte pineapple, and Dole celery. More savings for me! My total for my fruits and veggies for the week is just $4.39.

There are always frozen items on sale. Birds Eye has been offering many new varieties of vegetable mixtures, and new product introductions are always heavily couponed. I have three coupons for $1.50 off Birds Eye Steamfresh vegetables, and I spot them on sale for $1.59 per package. My final cost: 27¢ for all three. Lean Cuisine is featured in a half-price sale of $1.64 each. My coupon says $1 off four. My final cost is $5.56, or about a 60% savings off the regular retail.

Last stop before the checkout is meat. Perdue chicken breasts are on sale for $1.99 a pound, which I combine with my $1 Perdue coupon to pay just 99¢ a pound. Before I get to the checkout, I notice the Oscar Mayer hot dogs display boasting a special sale of 88¢ each. I check my coupon file, and I have one for $1 off two packages of the very same franks. For 38¢ a pack, hot dogs will be a weekend menu item.

So how did I make out? Well, let's do the math. In the end, I bought two bottles of mustard, two bottles of BBQ sauce, two packages of dog treats, four boxes of cereal, one stick of deodorant, nine bottles of detergent, four yogurts, a week's salad greens and fruit, three bags of frozen vegetables, four frozen dinners, one pound of chicken, and two packs of hot dogs. Without store sales and coupons, my total would have come out to right around $134.63. How much was my grand total? How about $36.83, for a total savings of $97.80, or 73%! Oh, and don't forget about my free T-shirt from Kellogg's with the mail-in rebate! More on rebates in the next chapter.

And that's all there is to it! I hope you enjoyed this little "walk down the aisle" with me—your friendly neighborhood Coupon Queen. Before I close this chapter, I want to talk briefly about some special programs you can enjoy at most of your local markets, drugstores, hardware stores, and other large chain vendors.

• • •

LOYALTY AND REWARDS PROGRAMS

· · · · · · · · ·

A few months ago my son Adam went to Staples to purchase several items he needed for his in-home office. He bought himself a new printer, several ink cartridges (black and color), folders, binders, reams of paper, and a whole host of pens, pencils, highlighters, and the like.

How much did he pay?

Nothing.

Yes, that's right. A brand-new printer and tons of essential supplies, absolutely free. How did he do it? He simply took advantage of the rewards program Staples offers to all customers: bring in a used printer cartridge, and get a $3 credit at the store at the end of the month. Adam had just left his previous job and gathered dozens of used cartridges that were going to be thrown out. Adam, however, is the son of the Coupon Queen, and he knew better than to let those empty cartridges go to waste. He brought them to the store three at a time, every day (the maximum amount allowed at the time—now you can only bring back ten per month), and ended up with over $200 in store credit. Staples then mailed him certificates for the money, which he used (before they expired, of course!) to buy the supplies. He combined these certificates with another special ("recycle your old printer for a $50 savings on a new one") and walked out a happy guy.

This is a prime example of how well a store loyalty program can work for consumers. Most people don't like the idea of committing to a certain store long enough to obtain the rewards necessary for major buying power. We haphazardly shop at a number of shops, and if we find we have a few dollars in credit for our months of shopping, then great. But we do not *actively* seek out these opportunities. I believe this to be a big mistake.

As I've said, retailers and manufacturers *want* us to take advantage of their offers, because it means we are buying their products with some degree of frequency. This is not the same, mind you, as blind store or brand loyalty, but rather a means of using the stores' programs to their fullest without feeling obligated to one over another. After all, as we discussed in step 2, you should end up with only a handful of stores you regularly shop at, perhaps two or three at most, and if you collect those stores' loyalty cards, you can make quite a killing!

And let us not forget about non-grocery stores. Drugstores, hardware stores, and home stores are now offering just as many coupons as grocery stores do. We have talked a lot about saving on household products like food and toiletries, but I have to point out how savings can also be yours on many other products. As with grocery coupons, most of these can be found on manufacturers' websites (I listed several in chapter 3). Staples is one example of a store that offers a fantastic recycling program. Not only is exchanging printer cartridges good for the environment, but it can net monstrous savings as well. It would take an entire book to list all of the fantastic new programs available to consumers now, but it is worth it to mention a few of the major ones here.

Rite Aid's Single Check Rebates

Literally hundreds of dollars in savings are offered each month through Rite Aid's Single Check Rebates program. Register your receipts and receive monthly rebate checks.

❖ Recent examples: Up to $10 rebate on Band-Aids, Neosporin, and Tylenol . . . $5 rebate on 24-count or larger Claritin allergy relief pills . . . up to $7.20 on GE bulbs.

Walgreens's Register Rewards

This program offers dozens of valuable instant rebates on health and beauty products each month. Printable coupons also are available on the website.

❖ Recent examples: Free Axe shampoo or conditioner, up to $6.99 . . . free Aquafresh 6 oz. toothpaste.

CVS's ExtraCare Rewards

Get 2% back on most purchases and an extra $1 back for each two prescriptions you fill at CVS. In addition weekly extra care bucks abound. CVS also offers printable online coupons on its website.

❖ Recent examples: $1.50 off All laundry detergent, 96 loads or larger size . . . $1 off Bausch & Lomb Renu fresh multi-purpose solution . . . $5 in Extra Bucks with the purchase of $15 in Energizer purchases (on sale for $5.99 for the 8-pack, and an extra $1 off with an on-package peel-off coupon).

Ace Hardware's Ace Rewards

Here you get 10 points for each $1 you spend at the store, with $5 off your next purchase for every 2,500 points earned ($250 spent). You start with 1,000 free bonus points just for signing up.

The Gap

Shop at the Gap (or a sister store, Old Navy or Banana Republic), then visit the website shown on your receipt. Fill out a quick survey and you'll earn a 10% discount off your next purchase. And recently I was mailed an additional 30% off coupon, one for The Gap, and a separate mailing for Old Navy.

Again, there are dozens of others, and I have listed only a few here. Other examples of stores that offer excellent deals like these include Best Buy, Bed Bath & Beyond, True Value Hardware, Petco, Lowe's, and Home Depot, to name just a few. Check out their websites and look for special deals. If you find anything interesting, be sure to drop me a line and let me know so I can help spread the word to other Supershoppers out there!

STORE CARDS

Similar to the rewards programs, store cards are a means by which the store is able to give the customer something back for buying. Not only that, but it is able to use these cards to track our buying habits and tailor our shopping experience accordingly. This helps the store tremendously, but it doesn't cost us a thing. By knowing what its shoppers are buying, a store can be sure to target those items and put them on sale more often. This allows them to see which products are simply not selling, and it gives them more insight into what we are looking for.

Besides the obvious advantage of having our local supermarket know what we like, consumer profiling, while maybe a bit high-tech and even sort of creepy in a sci-fi, "Big Brother is watching" kind of way, is great for us shoppers in other ways. We talked before about Catalina coupons, offers printed on the backs of our sales receipts (or printed separately) based on the purchases we have made during that shopping trip. The more we shop at a particular store, the more direct and targeted these coupons will be, and eventually technology will make it possible for us to see these Catalina coupons for every brand we buy with precise frequency based on how often we have bought a particular product.

Store cards are free just by filling out a quick form. If you are concerned about the safety of your information, it is true that there is no guarantee that the information you give is 100% secure. There have been cases of fraud involving store employees accessing customer information via these cards, but those cases are few and far between. In my opinion, it's as safe as it can be. In addition, very little information beyond name, address, phone, and email is ever asked for. Some chains will share customer information with "preferred partners," so information sharing can be a blessing and a curse. On the one hand, your information is being seen by multiple parties. On the other, this can be another means of ensuring yourself a frequent supply of home mailers with coupons inside that you can use. You may want to give a non-primary e-mail address on these card applications so that you don't have to rummage through tons of spam on your main account. Signing up for store cards is simple and the rewards can be great. Still, there are always risks to consider. Weigh the pros and cons and make your own decision based on what is best for you.

Most store cards work the same way: every time you make a purchase at Store A and have your card scanned, you will receive a small discount on the product. Right off the bat, you save some money. In addition, many cards tally your total purchase amount (during a specific time period) and reaching a certain amount will give you credit toward a future purchase or a free item, such as a holiday turkey or ham.

EXAMPLES OF STORE CARDS

Always be aware of how much the prices are being discounted. Oftentimes, a store that offers loyalty cards does so because it has upped the prices on products, so the "deal" you are getting is not truly a deal. As we have talked about almost ad nauseam by now, the key to being a successful Supershopper is being aware. If you note that the store you shop at that offers a loyalty card has prices much higher than a store that does not, it may be worth switching stores.

You don't need to bring all of your store cards with you every time you go shopping. Pick out the cards you will be using on a given trip and keep the rest aside, in alphabetical order by store name, for later use. Make sure you know where the cards are before entering the store, or at least by the time you get to the cash register, so you don't waste your time and everyone else's by fumbling around with your wallet, purse, or key chain for the right store card. Many stores can bring up your loyalty card number with just a phone number or zip code. Carrying actual cards may soon be a thing of the past.

And this brings us to my favorite part of Supershopping: watching those sales and coupons total up on the register; a little step I like to call . . .

CASHING IN AT THE CHECKOUT

People often ask me what the checkout people think about somebody who uses as many coupons as I do.

"Don't they shudder when they see you coming?" they ask. I guess people who don't use coupons regularly must feel a little guilty about doing it at all—as if they're somehow cheating the store out of something. And they must think stores dread a heavy couponer like me.

Well, I can assure you that this is not the way the stores see it. Nearly every store employee I've come into contact with as an advocate of Coupon Power has been polite, helpful, and eager to learn more about my system. Frequently, checkout people wish me continued good luck with my savings, and several of them have asked to subscribe to *Refundle Bundle*.

It's really to the stores' advantage to be cooperative, and as a result most store personnel are extremely courteous. After all, they want you back as a customer. It's in their best interests to have you satisfied.

Now, some of your fellow shoppers may not feel so gracious about it, especially if they pull in behind you just as you pull out a pack of cash-offs. I remember the poor man who scooted behind me the day we filmed the Betty Furness piece many years ago. All the other lanes had four or five customers in them, and he must have figured that, even with two cartloads of goods, I was a better act to follow than the others.

Unfortunately, he hadn't counted on my encore: the presentation of $123 worth of coupons. The expression on his face as the checker started to ring them up was one of the greatest double-takes I've ever seen.

Most shoppers, however, are pretty nice about it. They may grouse a bit for having to wait longer in line, but I've found that, when I talk to them, explaining what I'm up to, they're generally even more receptive than the employees. Which makes sense, because they've got a lot to gain by learning about Supershopping. It is important, of course, to be a considerate Supershopper, and take the necessary steps to ensure that the process is as seamless as possible. As a bonus, I check their cart to see if I can share my coupons. I always get a big thank-you and an even bigger smile when I can help someone save $4 or $5 off their grocery bill.

Help the cashier by keeping like products together.

Don't just dump everything down onto the conveyer belt. Stack items to get everything on as quickly as possible, and if you have ten or twenty of a certain product, just tell the number to the cashier so he or she doesn't have to scan each one individually.

Tell the cashier in advance you will be using coupons.

Sometimes stores have a special procedure in place for when a customer is using coupons. Be up-front, especially if you are going to be using a ton of coupons, so they know what they are getting themselves into and can call over a manager at the beginning if they are unsure how to handle the situation.

Have your coupons and loyalty card ready.

We have our at-home coupon organizer, right? Well, it might make sense either to buy a smaller one for actual shopping trips or to put all the coupons we are using that day in the *front* of our big file, in order to avoid shuffling through our entire folder in search of a 50¢ cash-off. Same goes for a store card. Have it out when you approach the register. It's just common sense, and common courtesy.

Keep an eye on the register.

Sometimes, not often, a computer will not have been properly updated with a store's sales for the week, especially earlier on in the week. Don't be shy about watching the numbers on the register to make sure they match what was advertised either in the circular or on the shelf. Also make sure your coupons are being scanned and processed correctly. Technology is definitely getting better, but even computers sometimes make mistakes. Don't be afraid to speak up! And check the receipt before leaving the store to get any errors corrected immediately.

Don't ask for double bagging unless you really need it.

It's simply wasteful to have several rolls of toilet paper double-bagged. For heavier products, of course it makes sense. But if you are parked near the store, the odds of the bag ripping are slim. Thousands of bags are wasted each year by shoppers, so please do your part by only double bagging if necessary. You can always take the cart to your automobile if you are parked far away. Even better: reusable bags are now popular, sometimes given away free or available for just 99¢ each.

The vast majority of people are more curious than annoyed when I walk up to the register. When they see how much I save by couponing, most of them turn from impatient to appreciative. I remember one woman in particular who was extremely skeptical as I laid a pile of coupons on the counter. She was, I guess, a typical Normal Shopper, the kind who feels that couponing is "just not worth the trouble."

"I cut those out once in a while," she said. "But I keep losing them, and they don't really save you very much anyway, do they?"

I introduced myself and assured her that, in fact, coupons can save you very much indeed, if you go about it right. Then, as the checker rang up my pre-coupon tally, I told her about *Refundle Bundle*, and I gave her my e-mail address to write to if she wanted to learn more about the system.

The total was something like $160. I saw my new friend glance at the register, then grin as I handed over the coupons. We chatted a bit more as the savings started being deducted. As the final total came up, I could see her eyebrows go up in surprise. When the checker announced, "Twenty-three dollars and ninety cents," there was another one of those double-takes that make Supershopping so much fun. The woman looked confused, then brightened and took out a pencil and paper.

"What was that address again?" she asked.

STEP 4:
SHOP SMART
·········

We've covered a lot in this chapter. Let's recap, shall we?

1. Resist impulse shopping.

I've said it before and I'll say it a hundred more times. Impulse buys are the number one cause of overspending for the average American consumer. The store has 1,001 ploys to get you to see every product inside in the hopes that you will buy something you don't truly need.

2. Have a walk-through plan beforehand.

Knowing how a store is laid out and being able to maneuver effectively through a store without repeating aisles or journeying into areas that are of no use to you will cut down on the likelihood of your making a poor shopping decision.

3. Don't be fooled by the store's tricks.

Stores take advantage of each of your five senses to lure you into buying their products. Ignore aromas, never shop while hungry, and be wary of supposed sales, introductory product offers, and bogus end-of-aisle "sales."

4. Use store cards and other loyalty programs—don't let them use you.

These free programs and cards are great if you are focused and understand the rules and rewards. But if the store cards are obligating you to shop at one chain at the expense of finding the best sales, then you are doing something wrong.

5. Be a considerate Supershopper.

Some people may be self-conscious about using coupons; you may feel even more uncomfortable when people are waiting in line behind you. Make things easier for everyone by being ready when you get to the register. Have your coupons out and your store rewards card ready. If you get stares, smile and explain what you're doing. I guarantee your fellow shoppers (and cashiers—they're shoppers, too!) will want to hear all about it. And if you have a coupon for an item in the cart of the person behind you, share; you'll bring smiles all around.

And there you have it! We have made it through the supermarket with me as your guide and saved a bundle on our groceries! I trust my little tour helped you out, as did the other tips. We're not done yet, though! We're about to delve into the fifth and final step of the Supershopping system, the part that happens *after* we've left the store!

STEP 5:

Aggressive Saving

·····································

Money in the Mail

W**HEN I FIRST** started developing the Supershopping system, Steve and I were working extra jobs to help pay our bills. Although we were both teachers, our salaries always fell short. Steve organized a drivers' education program for a private school, and I worked in an after-school program teaching arts and crafts. We barely had enough to pay the mortgage on our first house, and every day was a struggle. For years, saving money looked like some fairy-tale dream: something that, no matter how hard we tried, would always remain just beyond our grasp.

How is it, then, that we are now able to live comfortably? The answer lies in step 5 of my Supershopping system: a tax-free savings plan called refunding.

While coupon clipping has enabled me to cut our shopping bill in half for the past several years, refunding has given us a secure and steady fund of emergency money that has made it possible for us to realize some of our "impossible" dreams.

. . .

HOW YOU BENEFIT BY REFUNDING

Like couponing, refunding is a promotional tool the food manufacturers devised to get shoppers to try, and keep on buying, their products. Like coupons, refunds (or "rebates," as some refunders call them) are a simple and certain way of saving money at the supermarket. Like couponing, effective refunding relies on daily clipping, using national brands exclusively, and occasionally buying in bulk.

There are, however, major differences between step 3 and step 5 of the system.

First, while coupons are redeemed in the store at the time you buy the product, a refund will come to you in the form of a check or free product coupon, usually some weeks after you've sent in for it.

Second, you can realize savings with coupons merely by presenting them, and them alone, at the time of purchase, while many refund offers require you to mail in not only a proof of purchase but also a refund form (or "required blank") as well, before you can receive your check. See a sample refund offer on the next page.

Finally, the face value of most coupons is between 75¢ and $1; it's a rare cash-off that discounts over $2 (unless you're doubling). Refunds, on the other hand, generally *start* around $1.50, and can run as high as $20 for the cash offers (which we will delve into in a moment). As a matter of fact, in a single month I average about $200 in cash refunds or about $2500 a year. My postage costs come out of this fund. A hobby that actually pays you, unbelieveable. The free product coupons are another great by-product of refunding. My *free* DiGiorno Flatbread Melt coupon is valued at $3.99. So although refunding takes a little more time than coupon clipping, the extra savings make it well worth it.

SAMPLE REFUND OFFERS

TRY ME FREE*
*cash rebate by mail

organix
beauty pure and simple

TRY ME

vitaminshampoo

BUY: Any VitaminShampoo OR VitaminConditioner between 08/01/08 through 12/31/09.
SEND: This original form along with an original dated store-identified receipt with the VitaminShampoo or VitaminConditioner product price circled. Submission must be postmarked within 30 days of your purchase date.
RECEIVE: Up to $6.99 Cash Rebate (check will be for the qualifying product purchase price paid excluding sales tax. Maximum rebate value not to exceed $6.99).

SEND TO: CMS Rebate Center
Promo ID Vitamin001
P.O. Box 426006
Del Rio, TX 78842-6006

Name:_____

Address:_____
(Requests from P.O. Boxes will not be honored, acknowledged or returned)

City:_____

State:_____ Zip:_____

Date of Purchase:_____

Email:_____

There is such a thing as a FREE lunch.
IT'S NOT TAKEOUT. IT'S DIGIORNO.

NEW! DiGIORNO
FLATBREAD MELTS

Tombstone® Helps Pay Your Bills

MAIL-IN OFFER FORM/NOT PAYABLE AT RETAIL STORE. THIS MAIL-IN OFFER FORM MUST ACCOMPANY REQUEST.

1 • Purchase Seven (7) 12" Tombstone Pizzas and receive a $5 credit.
or
• Purchase Twelve (12) 12" Tombstone Pizzas and receive a $10 credit.
or
• Purchase Seventeen (17) 12" Tombstone Pizzas and receive a $15 credit.

2 Send this Offer Form and UPCs in a stamped envelope, and mail it to **Tombstone Helps Pay Your Bills, P.O. Box 19334, Irvine, CA, 92623-9334.** Your request must be postmarked by 01/15/10. Mail-in offers must be received by 02/01/10. To ensure payment to the correct account, please mail a copy of your utility statement.

3 Receive a $5, $10, or $15 credit on your next listed utility bill.*

PLEASE CHECK ONE:
☐ Home Heating   ☐ Utility
☐ Mobile Phone   ☐ Cable
☐ Satellite Movie

Utility Provider:_____ Account Number:_____

Name:_____
(Please Print)

Address:_____ Apt. #:_____
(Requests from P.O. Box Addresses will not be honored or returned)

City:_____ State:_____ Zip:_____

E-mail Address:_____

☐ I'd like to receive e-mail and/or mail communications such as recipes, access to offers, and product samples from KRAFT and/or its portfolio of brands.

Do you have a child under the age of 18? ☐ Yes ☐ No

What is the age range of the head of household? ☐ 18–34 ☐ 35–54 ☐ 55–64 ☐ 65+

Visit www.tombstone.com/payyourbills for further program details.

*Credit will be issued within 6–8 weeks of receipt of mail-in request.

UPC SAMPLE
1 2 3 4 5 6 7 8 9

09-05 335754

REQUESTS MUST BE RECEIVED BY 02/01/10. CREDIT WILL BE ISSUED IN 6 TO 8 WEEKS. LIMIT ONE REQUEST PER FAMILY OR ADDRESS. Offer good in USA, its territories and military addresses. Void where taxed, restricted or prohibited. Proofs of purchase submitted by clubs or organizations will not be honored or returned. Limit one Offer Form per envelope. Requests must be forwarded in an envelope with sufficient first class postage. Resellers of Kraft Foods products are excluded. Kraft Foods reserves the right to verify identification. No name and address labels accepted. Theft, diversion, reproduction, transfer, sale or purchase of this Offer Form, proofs of purchase or cash register receipts is prohibited and constitutes fraud. Fraudulent submissions could result in federal prosecution under the U.S. Mail Fraud Statutes (18 United States Code, Sections 1341 and 1342). ©2009 KF Holdings. Bill-Pay Bucks™ is a trademark of TPG Rewards, Inc.

Here's how refunding works:

1. The manufacturer issues an offer of a refund to all customers who have bought a particular product.

2. You, the shopper, take one of the refund forms, fill it out, and mail it in to the address given, accompanied by whatever proofs of purchase are required.

3. The form, with your proof of purchase, reaches its destination, which is generally not the manufacturer but an organization known as a redemption agency or clearinghouse, which processes the refund in the manufacturer's name.

4. The clearinghouse checks that you have sent the proper labels, panels, or other proofs to qualify for the offer—proofs of purchase, in fact, are often referred to as "qualifiers." Then it mails you a check or free product coupon in the manufacturer's name.

This whole process usually takes about four to eight weeks, from the time you mail off your qualifiers to the time the post office delivers your check or coupon.

That's it in a nutshell. You buy a product. You save the carton. You send it in to the company's representative. And they pay you for having bought it.

REALIZING THE BIGGEST DIVIDENDS

That is how refunding works on its own, and it can be extremely profitable even if used just by itself, but you'll realize the greatest savings if you use it in conjunction with couponing, as described in step 3. The beauty of Supershopping as a system is that all of its steps lock together to form a profitable whole. The expert couponer is the most likely candidate to earn big dividends as a refunder, and vice versa.

Regular refunding, combined with couponing, can sometimes make you feel a little embarrassed at how well you're doing. When you refund as often as I do, you soon find yourself on numerous mailing lists and are constantly opening envelopes full of cash-offs, two-for-one coupons, certificates for free samples—all of this in addition to the regular, daily refund checks.

Keep in mind that there are two types of "refunds" we are discussing now. The checks I am referring to are one kind; this is literal money back from the companies as a thank-you for buying and as partial reimbursement for the product purchased. There are also free product coupons, which can substitute for a money-back check; these are coupons (sent to your house once you have mailed in the form and qualifiers) that are good for a free package of another product, similar to the one you originally bought. Thus, I might buy three containers of Land O'Lakes butter, send in the UPCs as a proof of purchase (more on this below) and a refund form, and receive a coupon for a free container of Land O'Lakes Light butter. There are certain products, as a result, that I haven't laid out much money for in years—among them, spaghetti sauce, toilet tissue, paper towels, cereals, and various kinds of candy.

Money, of course, is the bottom line. It's hard to describe the pleasure a new refunder feels when she opens the mailbox and discovers that first refund check. I got my first one—a $1 rebate for buying Del Monte canned goods—about forty years ago, and I can still recall the delight of feeling that I was on to something important. How important, I didn't even imagine. I certainly never thought, as I admired that "thanks for buying" money from Del Monte, that within a few years I would be receiving enough similar checks to finance a Florida vacation!

Many of my 97% savings Supershopping trips result from combining store sales with these free product coupons and high-value manufacturer coupons that I received thanks to my refunding. It is a wonderful cycle of saving that I have been spinning in happily for years.

I already mentioned how strange it is that so few coupons are redeemed out of the billions issued. What is even stranger is how few shoppers are wise to the advantages of refunding. Even though their redemption rate is low, most American shoppers still do use coupons on at least a casual basis. You would think that a system that guarantees you will receive checks almost daily in the mail would gain at least as many converts. But for some reason that isn't so.

Everybody has heard of coupons, but when I talk to other shoppers about refund offers, I very seldom sense more than a dim appreciation of what I'm talking about. Yet the refunding system, as you've seen, is not complicated at all. Why do so few people use it?

The major reason, I suspect, is simply that most people still don't know about it. Coupons are hard to miss. They wave at us from every magazine, every newspaper, every specially marked package in the land. Refunds, on the other hand, are fairly obscure. Many shoppers don't even recognize a refund form when they see one. And many forms, sad to say, disappear from the stores before their time because of limited distribution.

But there are other reasons for their lack of popularity. Some shoppers are under the mistaken notion that cashing in with refunds involves buying truckloads of items you don't want. Others, without ever trying the system, presume that anything that guarantees you a steady extra income must be either a lot of trouble or illegal.

Neither of these suppositions is correct. What I want to do in the remainder of this chapter is to outline my refunding system in some detail, clearing up the misconceptions and explaining how refunding brings me approximately $2,500 *each year* in tax-free extra income and *free* coupons that add to my 50%–65% grocery savings each week.

How can refund money be tax-free? The IRS looks at money sent to you for having bought a certain brand of product not as income, but as a reduction in the purchase price of the articles purchased. It makes no distinction between coupons and refund checks, to our great advantage.

THREE EASY STEPS:
THE REFUNDER'S S.O.S.

·········

If you're like I was before I developed my system, you sometimes feel financially as if you're on a desert island with very little food or water. Well, couponing can be a way of making the available supplies stretch, but refunding can be the means that finally rescue you. To make it work properly, however, you have to follow what I call "the Refunder's S.O.S."

Just as the dedicated couponer can realize savings far in excess of those realized by the casual clipper, so, too, can the dedicated refunder profit enormously if he or she approaches refunding not so much as a hobby (although it is a fascinating one) but as a matter of immediate financial aid. I know it was the combination of coupons and refunding that bailed us out of our financial bind years ago. When you're stranded on a desert island, you can't just thrash your arms about and scream wildly, hoping someone will hear you. You've got to go about rescuing yourself in as cool and organized a manner as possible, or you'll simply end up getting hoarse.

At the risk of straining my metaphor to the breaking point, let me share the three steps of the Refunder's S.O.S.

S: **Save** everything you can find that might help you.
O: **Organize** your time and labor as efficiently as possible, to make the best use of what you find.
S: **Send** out messages for help—bottles, smoke signals, bonfires—on a regular, consistent basis.

S: Save Everything: It's Valuable

In the last section I mentioned proofs of purchase and said that, in order to get cash refunds, you have to send them in along with the relevant rebate forms. Actually, when refunders talk about proofs of purchase, they mean two things.

One definition of proof of purchase is a sticker or section of a package that actually contains the phrase "proof of purchase" or something similar, such as "purchase confirmation" or "purchase seal." Such a seal—generally enclosed within a dotted line—is put on packages specifically to serve as your proof of having bought the product.

But there is another, broader definition of proof of purchase. Manufacturers sometimes change the part of their packaging that they will accept as proof of purchase, and you may find that such other parts of a box as the net weight statement, the box top (or bottom), the ingredients panel, the tear strip, or the Universal Product Code (UPC) seal are requested in refund offers in lieu of the actual proof of purchase seal. In these cases, whatever part of the packaging is requested is really being used as a proof of purchase. To avoid confusion between the specific and the general use of the term, refunders usually refer to any packaging part being requested as a *qualifier*, and they reserve use of the term "proof of purchase" to mean the actual proof of purchase seal. The point to remember here, though, is that you can never tell when you buy a product which part of its packaging will eventually be required as a qualifier.

Thus, if you really want to profit from refunding, you must save *everything*. Since you don't know what part of a box will later qualify you for a dollar back, you simply have to keep the whole thing, and cut off the relevant portions when the time comes. The same rule should apply to bottles: save not only the front labels, but also the neck labels and the cap liners or inner seals. With canned goods, save the entire label.

In addition, the wise refunder also saves his or her cash register receipts. Companies may ask you to provide the original or a copy of your sales slip, with the relevant purchase price circled, as an extra proof that you have in fact bought the product.

Naturally, saving everything means that at any one time you are likely to have on hand a huge stash of packaging and packaging parts. But you need not feel as if you're living in a paper recycling plant if you follow a few simple guidelines.

First, try to make your qualifiers as small as possible. The method I use with boxes (such as cereal and detergent boxes) is to remove the inner wrapper (companies seldom ask for that since it has no identifying marks), then peel off the thick cardboard backing until I'm left with the outer covering alone: the part with the writing on it. A sharp knife or razor is helpful here, although your fingernails will do just about as well. (Other refunders have found that wetting the box and letting it sit in a large plastic bag overnight makes the front covering even easier to peel off.)

Finally, I flatten down this emaciated outer layer of the box until it's the thickness of just a couple of pieces of typing paper, and I put a rubber band around groups of them to secure them. This makes them a lot easier to store.

With cans and bottles you simply steam or soak off the labels in hot water. With bottle caps keep the liners if there is something identifiable on it and recycle or redeem bottles themselves. Many states have excellent systems in place for both options.

Peeling off cardboard backings and soaking off labels may not be your idea of a high old time, but it's surprising how quickly you can get to like the chore when you know there's money in it for you.

14 OZ HONEY NUT CHEERIOS UPC SYMBOL #

0 16000 66590 3

5M-642

0 12000 80999 6

PROOF OF PURCHASE

Keebler® Fudge Shoppe®
Deluxe Grahams 12.5 oz.
UPC Proof of Purchase

0 30100 01610 6

Benadryl

ALLERGY

Proof of Purchase

3 12547 17031 4

13 OZ PCP
PROOF-OF-PURCHASE

0 43000 12951 7

0401385590000

© KRAFT FOODS

COCOA PEBBLES®
CEREAL BRAND

SHEER PLEASURES-GREEN
SIMPLES PLAISIRS-VERT

0 36000 29130 8

Kleenex® BRAND
TISSUE

Many refunders even manage to have fun doing it. One refunder in Colorado, whom I met through *Refundle Bundle*, has made a regular Saturday morning ritual of label soaking and box slicing—with the whole family involved. She and her husband peel off cardboard backings while their two children slosh the empty bottles around in the sink. To them it's a game, but at the end of an hour or so of soaking in warm soapy water, the labels come off easily. Then the kids stick them up against the inside of the kitchen cabinets (glue side facing out), where the damp labels adhere until they are dry and ready for storage.

Which brings me to the *O* part of my refunding S.O.S.—organizing the qualifiers into a compact and workable storage space, where they can stay until they're ready to make you money.

O: Organize with These Easy Secrets

Now that you have all those qualifiers, where on earth will you put them?

The most common complaint I hear from new refunders is that their living space is being gobbled up by packaging. "It's like I'm living in a blizzard of qualifiers," one woman said to me. "I have so many of the things, I can't put my finger on the one I want when I want it."

I asked this woman what kind of filing system she used, and she stared at me as if she were puzzled.

"Why, I don't have any special system, I guess. Some are on my counter, some are in canisters, and . . . well, I just never thought about filing them."

"Think about it," I advised. And I explained to her the importance of organization.

At any one time I probably have up to a thousand different

qualifiers in my house, ready to be tapped when needed. My memory is pretty good, but I'm certainly not so foolhardy as to rely on that alone to keep track of that many box tops, seals, and labels. Over the years, experience has taught me that the refunder who makes the most money is the one who can find any required qualifier as soon as it's needed, without having to turn the house upside down in the process. This means that, if you're going to negotiate step 5 successfully, you'll need a workable filing system.

It need not be elaborate. Very few refunders, I would guess, are certified public accountants on the side; few of us can afford to be bothered with shelves of ledgers, in-and-out baskets, and other paraphernalia. But we all understand that the sooner we can dig up our proofs, the sooner we'll get that check.

My filing system is, I think, fairly typical of other refunders' systems. All it takes is a plastic produce bag, a few shoe boxes, and one large envelope.

> **My filing system is, I think, fairly typical of other refunders' systems. All it takes is a plastic produce bag, a few shoe boxes, and one large envelope.**

The plastic bag I keep in a drawer, and whenever I get a bunch of qualifiers, I toss them in until I'm ready to file them. Generally it takes three or four weeks until the bag is full, and at that point I haul it out and go to my shoe boxes.

I have six of these—half of them boot size—plus one large box (24 x 18 x 10 inches). All are kept out of the way in the garage. In the regular-sized shoe boxes I file my flattened-down qualifiers, arranged alphabetically according to product name. In the three boot boxes I keep qualifiers arranged according to type of product, since for certain items this seems an easier method for me. In the first boot box I have margarine boxes, cream cheese boxes and wrappers, and cocoa and noodle boxes. I know that may seem an eccentric combination, but it works for me. In the second boot box I file qualifiers from toothpaste, pizza, batteries, drugs, and plastic bags such as Glad and Hefty. In the third one I keep qualifiers from frozen foods, coffee, cereals, crackers, candy, frozen cakes, cookies, and disposable cups.

Finally, I have the one large box, about two feet long and a foot and a half wide. It holds salad dressing labels, soap wrappers, detergent boxes, tea boxes, paper towel wrappers, and labels from plastic bottles.

That's the entire system. Six shoe boxes and one larger box, arranged with a combination of alphabetical regularity and (I admit) personal caprice. But I'm so thoroughly familiar with what I have that I never have to hunt for what I want.

Many new refunders worry that a file such as this will take up so much space that their families will have to sleep on the roof. They needn't worry. My entire shoe box operation takes up only about four square feet of floor space, and some refunders who are even more strapped for space than we are make even more efficient use of small areas.

Still, many people simply cannot find the time to organize that many qualifiers and simply give up on the whole process altogether. If you find yourself tight on space (and time), follow this rule of thumb: ignore everything but the UPCs, because nowadays most manufacturers ask only for UPCs of the products and nothing else. Either way, you should hang on to your UPCs—and be absolutely certain to label the backs of them since you will have no other way of keeping track of what is what.

You also want to keep track of your refund forms. These I keep in a single large business envelope, filed alphabetically by product and with the expiration date circled. Since I only have about one hundred of these at any one time, and since I check them frequently, it's never a problem finding the ones I want.

Many refund offers are now found on the Internet. Inside *Refundle Bundle* I have six or more pages of them, totaling over one hundred offers. These offers change each issue, and on our discussion board at www.CouponQueen.com are daily postings of new offers.

Some refunders prefer to use a small filing box for forms, and some like to file them chronologically according to expiration date. Either of these techniques is fine, and you should use whatever system works for you. You'll know it's working if you can pull together the appropriate forms and qualifiers without upending the house—and if you can do so consistently, without finding that three-quarters of them have expired.

One way I avoid this is to pull selected forms as their expiration dates approach and paper-clip them onto whatever qualifiers I have toward the offer. I keep these packets that are nearing their expiration dates in a top kitchen drawer, and as I acquire new proofs, I simply add them to the packets rather than file them in my shoe boxes. This way I keep down to a bare minimum the number of "passed ED" disappointments.

Some manufacturers require, in addition to a qualifier or proof of purchase, a dated cash register receipt to verify the purchase. I file these by dates in an envelope. In the event I have more than one offer on a receipt, I request a substitute receipt or duplicate which many stores can print out easily. At a recent trip to CVS I had two refunds during the same shopping trip: a full-price refund on Organix Shampoo and a second on Spot Shot, both requiring a receipt. The clerk gave me a substitute receipt and I was good to go.

One more aspect to refunding organization you may want to consider is keeping a running record of what refunds you have sent away for, and when. Many refunders keep such a log to be able to check up on the companies periodically and see whether there are any outstanding refunds that they might reasonably expect in short order. They arrange their logs in column order in a notebook, with a heading for the company name and address, what qualifiers were sent and when, and the name and amount of the refund. As the checks come in, they mark them off in a final "Received" column. See the next page for an example of such a log.

There's nothing wrong with keeping this kind of record, and if you have the time and inclination, I say go right ahead. Certainly it provides you with a quick and accurate way of determining who owes you what—and of seeing, over time, how much money you've made on refunding. It also teaches you which companies are the most prompt in sending refunds.

But personally, I don't find record keeping necessary. The companies have always been quite considerate with me, and since only a small fraction of refund requests go astray in the mail, I don't feel it's worth my time to check up on all of them. I suppose I must lose track of some offers this way, but probably not enough to make much of a dent in that yearly $2,500. When I send in for a refund, I like to forget about it until it arrives—at which time it's like a pleasant surprise.

But to be "surprised" like this on a daily basis, you have to practice, without fail, the final part of my Refunder's S.O.S. You must send in for those checks.

Refund Log Sheet

COMPANY	ADDRESS OF REFUND	DATE SENT	DATE RECEIVED	AMOUNT	COMMENTS

S: Send Away for Refunds Regularly

Sending for your money on a regular, consistent basis is very important. No matter how well managed your filing is, it will do you no good unless you make it a point to ask for your checks and free product coupons as often as offers become available and you have the necessary qualifiers. I send out about one hundred letters a month.

"Doesn't that take a lot of time?" I'm often asked.

In fact, it doesn't. The *total* amount of time I spend on refunding—this includes clipping, filing forms, arranging qualifiers, *and* sending for the offers—never exceeds four or five hours a week. That's less than an hour a day. To make life even easier, manufacturers have recently begun offering online refunds—no mailing required!

There are plenty of ways to cut down on refunding time if you are not tech-savvy and choose not to use the online refunding method. It's easy to cut corners on the actual sending part of the process, like using return address labels. I do most of my filling in of forms and addressing of envelopes, for example, while I'm also doing something else: riding in the car, watching television, or just waiting for the water to boil. When I play mahjongg, I address envelopes when it's my turn to be out. Before long, addressing ceases to be a chore and becomes, like knitting, something to keep my hands busy.

The main thing to remember about the time spent on refunding is that, if you start to see it as drudgery, you'll soon defeat the purpose of the game. After all, it ought to be fun to save. If you arrange your time so that addressing envelopes is something you do along with something else, before you know it you'll have fifty forms in the mail, and be on your way to becoming $100 richer next month.

Beyond that, here are a couple of points to keep in mind as you write the companies.

1. Be sure that whatever qualifiers you're sending are precisely the ones they've requested. If an offer calls for the net weight seals from two small-sized boxes of dog food, the company generally will not honor the seal from one (or even two) large-sized boxes. A refunder friend from North Carolina was recently refused a refund because she sent the dog food manufacturer the label from puppy food when the offer had specified "adult dog food." There are occasional exceptions, but in general you must give them exactly what they ask for, or you'll be out of luck.

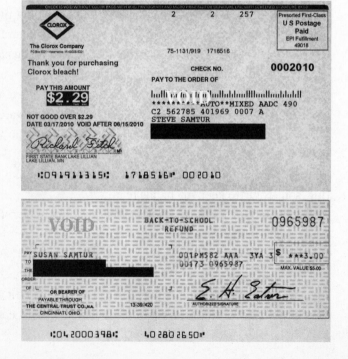

P&G Pharmaceuticals
P.O. Box 42485 Cincinnati, OH 45242-0485

56-91
422

First Financial Bank NA,
Hamilton, Oh 45011

| 07-08-2009 | 113231 | $********20.00 |

PAY ********************************20 DOLLARS 00 CENTS

TO THE ORDER OF   Susan Samtur

EXPIRES 90 DAYS AFTER ISSUE DATE.

⑈113231⑈ ⑆04220091⑆ 531027374 2⑈

DIAGEO

www.thebar.com

PO Box 1750
Winston-Salem, NC 27102-1750

CITIZENS STATE BANK
CLARA CITY, MN 56222   709757   75-485/919

DIAGEO0021 80120   90002 RW30128305

CHECK NO.   319076
DATE   03/29/2010

Void after 180 days

AMOUNT $25.00

VOID

REBATE FOR PURCHASE FROM DIAGEO SPIRITS
PAY TWENTY FIVE DOLLARS AND 00/100

TO THE ORDER OF
STEPHEN SAMTUR

⑆091904856⑆   709757⑈ 319076

027624

35-1126
912

HELLMANNS/BEST FOODS REBATE   P.O. BOX 848
GRAND RAPIDS, MN 55744

FIRST-CLASS MAIL
PRESORTED
U.S. POSTAGE PAID
GRAND RAPIDS, MN
PERMIT NO. 231

FIRST NATIONAL BANK OF COLERAINE
COLERAINE, MN 55722

TO THE ORDER OF

VOID IF NOT CASHED

**********************AUTO**MIXED AADC 556
R5569-R004716 5 7 1562 -10657 -   MAAD MAA MB
S SAMTUR

PAY $*3.19
NOT GOOD FOR
MORE THAN: $*3.19

VOID

⑆091217200⑆ 8319001639⑈ 027624

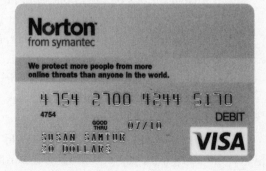

2. Before you send the form in, check to see that it has not expired. This will avoid your receiving one of those disheartening letters that begins, "We regret to inform you . . ." Once in a while a company, to keep itself in your good graces, will extend an offer beyond the date printed on the form; it may do this especially if the closing date is near. But extension is not something you can count on, so you should be careful about keeping an eye on those EDs before the date gets too close.

3. Be patient. Many novice refunders have complained to me that their refunds "just aren't coming." Hold on a while; they will. The clearinghouses have to process a large volume of forms, and as a result, getting your money can sometimes take even more time than the forms themselves indicate it will. Don't give up. The companies are, almost without exception, quite honorable in their dealings with refunders, and unless you have waited in vain for, say, three or four months, I'd advise you not to write them a letter of complaint. If you simply can't wait any longer, a brief, polite note stating the name of the refund and the date you sent it in will get you your refund a lot faster than an attack on their policies or integrity. Send it to the Customer Service Department of the company that offered the refund. Better yet, check the package for the toll-free number and give the company a call. You can also contact the company via e-mail. I have found all companies to be very responsive.

That's my Refunder's S.O.S. You should always remember that the more work you put into this rewarding hobby, the less it will seem like a hobby and the more it will take on the attributes of a home-based moneymaking venture. Which, of course, is exactly what it is.

At the same time, you should not be putting so much work into it that it ceases to give you pleasure. I suppose that if I put in ten or twelve hours a week on refunding, I might be getting back several hundred dollars more a year than I am, and if you feel up to that kind of investment of time, it may prove worth your while. For me, less than an hour a day for $2,500 a year seems just about right, with the added bonuses of the free product coupons.

WHERE TO FIND THOSE ALL-IMPORTANT FORMS

Forms are available in all the places that coupons are available, plus a couple more. Listed here are the principal sources.

In Stores

There are two kinds of forms you can generally pick up at the supermarket. One type, called the "store form" ("SF" is the refunders' common abbreviation), is found attached to shelves in tear-off pads. If the forms are all gone, you can get the information for the form on the cardboard backing. The cardboard backing will ask you to send your name and address plus the qualifiers to the address provided to receive *either* the refund itself or the form to send in for the refund. Cardboard backings are very important for refunders. For that reason you should avoid removing them from the shelves; leave them for the next shopper to see. Just jot down the relevant information, and you'll get your money in due order. For better distribution, some stores keep their forms in a central location, such as the courtesy desk. Ask to see these forms before shopping; it might influence your purchases.

Another type of in-store form is the kind that appears on the products themselves. These may be printed on the actual packaging itself, or they may be attached to it in the form of stickers or (in the case of bottles) "hang tags" (HTs). Sadly, hang tags have a way of disappearing rapidly, too, since people will often tear them off the bottle without buying the item. Remember, we're all in this to save money, so consideration is a goal as well as saving money.

In Newspapers and Magazines

Periodicals often contain forms good not only for cash refunds, but also for free coupons for products—on some household products these could be valued as high as $15. Check the Sunday supplements especially.

Via Home Mailers and Online Company Newsletters

By becoming an active refunder, you will almost certainly increase your chances of receiving forms (and coupons) through the mail. The quickest way I know to get on a refund mailing list is to send in for that first refund. In addition, online company newsletters are growing by leaps and bounds. By signing up online (most require less than a minute to register), you will receive information on coupon acquisition, online refunds, and other special promotions.

• • •

From the Companies

Let's say your local supermarket has been the victim of one of those form hoarders I mentioned earlier, and that someone else has used the cardboard backing to obtain a store form. You can still write to the company directly to request a form; remember to address your letter to the attention of the Customer Service Department. All the major firms have such departments now, and they are usually extremely helpful to the "formless" refunder. Here, too, a toll-free call or e-mail will usually get you results.

By Trading with Others

Subscribing to a refunding newsletter is, without a doubt, the single best way to receive both information about current offers and the forms necessary to send in for them. The main advantage of belonging to the refunding network that operates through these bulletins is that it multiplies by many times the chances that you will spot, and thus be able to profit from, an available offer. When you get a monthly bulletin, you automatically enlist refunders from New York to California to search along with you, and this immediately increases your chances of catching the most lucrative offers. Newsletters also put you in contact with many people who may have forms that you lack, and these are people who are looking to trade them with you for the forms you have that *they* lack. By joining together, everybody profits.

You can take a look at a sampling of *Refundle Bundle* by going to my website www.refundlebundle.com. There you'll find specific offers, freebies, and great general information on how to refund.

Through Internet Offers

The fastest growing source of forms is the Internet. All companies have their own websites, and by clicking on the links to special offers or promotions, you'll find a wealth of deals geared toward the consumer. I recently printed off a form for a free Reynolds Wrap, a free Black & Decker Dustbuster from Procter & Gamble, and a full purchase price refund of up to $4.99 for All-Bran from Kellogg.

PREMIUMS

If I've given the impression up until now that refunders never think of anything but money, I'd like to correct it here.

Actually, money is only one of many benefits enjoyed by the devotees of Supershopping. It is also possible to receive such things as free samples of products, numerous coupon giveaways, and enough free merchandise—from toys to clothing to kitchen appliances—to keep your house looking like the holidays all year round.

> **Money is only one of many benefits enjoyed by the devotees of Supershopping**

I love these premiums because I bundle like items together in a lovely basket and use them for bridal showers, baby showers, and housewarming gifts. I complement the goodies with other similar household items to make well-rounded and useful gift baskets.

I recently attended a bridal shower, and here's what I did. I

bought a large pail and filled it with various household supplies that I had gotten for free or nearly free—detergent, fabric softener, spray starch, window cleaner, paper towels, Mr.
Clean, Clorox wipes, and toothpaste and toothbrushes that I
tied together with a pretty ribbon—and added a batch of useful coupons. I packaged the whole bucket and its contents
with cellophane wrap and a large bow for a perfect presentation. It made quite a hit. The retail value was over $50, my
cost under $10.

Many refunders are so attracted to the idea of receiving such
bonuses—refunders call them "premiums"—that they devote
the bulk of their savings time to acquiring them; I know more
than one refunder whose kitchen apparatus (dishes, utensils,
dish towels, and a hundred odds and ends) has been paid for by
the big food companies. Other refunders, while concentrating
on cash rebates or free product coupons, find the occasional
acquisition of premiums a good way to stock up on holiday and
birthday gifts; to them, premiums provide that extra something
that makes refunding more than just a steady diet of cash. (I
guess they get bored with all that money.)

"Absolutely Free"

It's amazing how many things in this country can be had for
practically nothing. The old advertising catchphrase "absolutely free" may not have the ring of absolute truth about it,
but when you start looking into supposedly free offers, you
find that it's often not far off the mark. For a nominal handling
fee and no proofs or purchase, you can acquire thousands of
manufacturers' giveaways. And in many cases the companies
don't even require the fee; they'll send you the item for literally nothing at all.

Walmart.com has a samples page. You can pick and choose those items you'd like to try. At no cost to you, these samples arrive in your mailbox. Dove is another company that offers lots of free things. Each new version of soap, liquid soap, body wash, and shampoo brings its own freebie. Go to the sites of some of your preferred companies, and you're bound to find many of these.

Manufacturers give things away for a good reason. They see their gifts both as a way of introducing themselves and their products to new customers and as a means of building good public relations. These particular giveaways don't require qualifiers, although more lavish gifts do. All you have to do for these is send your name and address to the companies, and wait. In most cases, all it takes is a postcard.

The active refunder has excellent opportunities to acquire things for free, because once you start clipping forms and getting yourself on mailing lists, the companies will knock themselves out trying to be the first to send you information about discounted and "absolutely free" items.

One of the most common types of freebies is the free sample. Manufacturers are continually giving away free bottles of bleach, boxes of cereal, and tubes of toothpaste to introduce you to new products and to find new customers for their established products. The discussion board of RefundleBundle.com has hundreds of these postings for all to share.

Manufacturers give away free products in several ways. Sometimes they simply mail all the residents of a given neighborhood actual samples of the product, in either a trial or a small size. At other times they prefer to catch you in the store and will distribute the samples at a special table or from a special display. Generally, this kind of promotion is advertised in the front of the store with posters and banners. And lately many freebies accompany the delivery of my Sunday newspaper.

More frequently, however, the companies give you coupons for samples rather than the samples themselves. You can find coupons for free products in all the places you find coupons in general: newspapers, magazines, and the stores. Even if the offer is only for a trial size, you'll save something by getting it free, and the wise shopper keeps an eye out for these freebie tickets. Probably everybody, Supershopper or not, has gotten a free sample at one time or another. The free sample giveaway is one of the most obvious and widely advertised devices that companies use to get us interested in their wares. But samples are by no means the only things they offer us. The range of freebies offered as rewards for buying is enormous. If you really concentrated on it, I bet you could probably get the companies to pay for practically everything in your house, aside from the bills and the furniture.

Premium giveaways work on the same principle as refunds. You buy a product and save the qualifiers. The manufacturer announces (in a magazine, on a package, in a mailer, or on the Internet) that you can get a given premium by sending in a specified number of qualifiers. You send them in, with an order form if it's required. Your order goes to a clearinghouse, and in a few weeks you are the owner of a new shirt, tote bag, coffee mug, or cigarette lighter. To this day I still use the Maxwell House thirty-cup coffeemaker I received over twenty years ago and the Tropicana beach towel that looks almost as good as the day it arrived in the mail. One of my newest acquisitions is a large cooler from Gatorade, great for our outdoor parties and picnics.

Cash-Plus Offers

When you consider that even many "absolutely free" deals require you to send a nominal handling fee in order to get your premium, I guess you could say that a lot of these offers are really only "relatively free"; technically. Still others not only request the handling fee but also a payment, they are "cash-plus" (or "money-plus") offers, meaning deals where the company specifically requests a cash payment (not simply a "postage and handling charge") in addition to proofs of purchase. Money-plus offers like this are quite common. For example, Kellogg gives away many freebies like a great limited edition alarm clock for six proofs of purchase and no charges. But on occasion it has items that we call money-plus. Its ESPN basketball requires two UPCs plus $8.99. This is an offer I'd pass up. Personally, I've never been fond of paying out cash to get anything that's being advertised as a free gift. There are so many really free offers around that it seems almost a waste of money to actually *pay* for a premium. For this reason I've generally excluded cash-plus offers from the pages of *RefundleBundle.com* and asked that my subscribers, when they write in to inform me of new offers, mention only those for which no money is required.

Naturally, there are exceptions, and if you don't happen to be as biased as I am against paying out cash (remember, this is a book about cashing *in*), you'll probably order more cash-pluses than I do. You probably won't be sorry, either. Generally the merchandise offered is almost always well worth the price being asked; and in many cases it's considerably below retail.

The best way to earn premiums is to shop where the prices are best, to buy only brand names, and to faithfully clip every coupon, label, and refund form in sight. Using my qualifiers for premiums as opposed to refunds may have made me miss out on potential cash flow into my bank account, but it's enabled me to fill my house with goodies from numerous companies, and to purchase occasional money-plus items that would be cheap at twice the price. Whether this system will be best for you I can't determine. For myself, I'm not complaining.

Some of my favorite freebies come from the cereal companies. Kellogg is probably one of the most generous companies. Recently for various "qualifiers" I got a free alarm clock, a camera, and a classic movie DVD. Tropicana.com is running a unique rewards program for buying its orange juice, and Coke has been offering an assortment of items at Mycokerewards. com. My neighbor is still wearing the Fanta T-shirt I gave him from that site.

In both the Coca-Cola and the Tropicana program, the more you buy, the more rewards you can get. Loyalty is what they're looking for.

STEP 5:
AGGRESSIVE SAVING

Here are the most important points to remember about refunds, the "extra mile" of the Supershopping system.

1. Enjoy your tax-free income.

Refunding, in which manufacturers reimburse you for buying, is a great addition to any Supershopper's diet. It can provide you with a substantial extra savings account. Typical refunds come either as checks from the manufacturer or free product coupons for your next purchase.

2. Look for refund offers.

You can find refund offers on specially marked packages, on store shelves, at supermarket courtesy booths, in newspapers and magazines, in home mailers, and on the Internet. Offers are also listed regularly in refunding newsletters. Just check the *Refundle Bundle* discussion board and you'll find daily postings of a plethora of great refunds.

3. Remember the Refunder's S.O.S.

Save the "proofs of purchase" for all your products along with the refund forms available at the stores, find a system for organizing them compactly, and send them out with frequency to make the most money from your efforts. By doing this on a consistent yet casual basis (much like couponing), you will slowly but surely realize great dividends without it feeling too much like work!

4. Be precise when you send in for refunds.

When you send in for offers, be sure that you include exactly what the offer asks for, and that it has not expired. Be patient: offers sometimes take a few months to be processed.

5. Send away for premiums.

By saving qualifiers regularly, you can acquire absolutely free merchandise (premiums) worth $10 to $20 or more. Among the most common offers are clothing, tools, small appliances, cookbooks, kitchen implements, and toys.

6. Take up cash-plus offers with care.

Some premiums are offered on a "cash-plus" or "money-plus" basis: the customer must send in money as well as qualifiers to get the gift. Even so, "cash-plus" premiums represent a great savings over the store price. Use these gifts at your discretion; don't get so wrapped up in it that you're spending all your hard-saved money on these offers!

And with that, we conclude the five-step Supershopping System. Congratulations! You're finally ready to make the most of your shopping experience and save over 50% or more of your monthly grocery bill. Before we conclude, let's do a quick summary of the five steps.

6

Putting It All Together

· ·

Supershopping: A System Summary

WE HAVE COVERED a lot in these pages, and I think we could all benefit from a review session. The Supershopping System is not a terribly complex program, but there are a lot of key points you should make sure you are taking away from this book. Everything else—the tips, tricks, and statistical info I have covered—is helpful for your knowledge as an alert shopper, but the actual steps involved in becoming a Supershopper are much more important.

Step 1 Review: Get into the Mindset

This may seem like a trivial step to you, while in fact this is the most crucial point for most Normal Shoppers, as it is the attitude we take toward shopping that keeps us mired in inflationary prices and subconscious marketing strategies. Becoming aware of the potential savings and walking into the supermarket with a positive, aggressive frame of mind is the surest way to guarantee yourself immense savings off that final total.

What's more, we have to shake the idea that coupons, refunds, and discounts will only shave off a few pennies from our bill. Looking at the short-term savings will not do us any good; we have to think of the Supershopping System in terms of an annual savings potential, and in terms of percentages. As I have mentioned, I can easily and regularly save 50%–65% of my weekly bill using this system, and while on any given trip that might "only" be $20 or $30, some days that 50%–65% looks more like $70 or $80. Multiply that by fifty-two weeks in a year, and we're talking as much as $4,000 in savings, not to mention all the money we will be getting back in refunds, which can total another $2,500 each year. Now, who was saying something about a week-long cruise through the Mediterranean?

Once we start looking at the program through these rosy lenses, we can start preparing ourselves to enter the supermarket. First, let's review the POP Blocks, the building blocks to step 1 of the Supershopping System.

1. *Plan ahead* by doing a full inventory of your house to figure out what items you need. This means more than just scouring your kitchen for food items; it means walking through the bathroom(s), laundry room, linen closet, and any other area of the house where grocery items are stored. How can we know if we need more Q-tips or fabric softener if we are looking in our fridge? Know how much your family needs in a given week and don't buy an excess of products, or else you'll end up throwing most of it away. Nonperishables are okay to buy in bulk, but only if the price is right. Keep all this in mind when you are taking stock at home, and stick to the items you will need *that week* (if this means planning meals to

know what products you will have to buy, then all the better—the first *P* in the POP Block does stand for *planning*, after all!). As I mentioned, a once-a-week, well-organized shopping trip will end up being the most efficient and effective in terms of saving both time and money, not to mention energy!

2. A list is crucial, or else we will end up walking in blind and grabbing items we don't really need. Having a list also keeps us focused on the task at hand and helps us break the habit of impulse shopping; that is, buying items on a whim. If you find yourself shopping on impulse, you are like most Normal Shoppers out there, and unfortunately, you'll be spending another 30%–40% on the items the store has tricked you into buying by using its clever psychological ploys.

3. Keep your list organized in categories the way the grocery store does it. This will help you when you enter the store as it will serve as your map to the supermarket itself, which as a general rule is unwieldy and complex.

4. *Organize yourself.* A well-thought-out list is only the first step. Pick up a coupon organizer and create a concrete filing system for yourself that will be easy for you to sort through. Do the same for your refund offers and qualifiers, and make sure the system you develop is not only consistent, but also compact. A huge garage full of qualifiers and coupons will not be of any help to you.

5. Don't forget to organize your *time* as well. Plan on doing your major shopping trip once a week, and spending around an hour in the store or stores. Chances are, as we mentioned earlier, you will be able to complete your trip in even less time (I am often in and out

in thirty minutes), but it's not a bad idea to allot extra time, especially when you're first starting out as a Supershopper. Break the habit of picking up all your items as you need them, since the more times we enter the grocery store, the more chances the store has to tempt us into making a few extra purchases, which in the end will really add up. Look forward to your weekly trip as an adventure and as an opportunity to save money, not as a chore or inconvenience.

6. *Practice makes permanent.* You are bound to have a learning curve and you won't start realizing 50% savings right away; it takes time and patience to develop into a master Supershopper, but once you are there, you'll never look back! Remember, it may take some time to build up your coupon file; don't expect an exhaustive collection of cash-offs and qualifiers overnight. Like any good system, Supershopping requires a bit of time and persistence.

7. Get yourself into a routine of clipping coupons, checking the Internet for coupons and sales, looking through store flyers for discounts, filing the coupons you have, and sending in for refunds. The more you do it, the less time it will take. Besides my weekly shopping trip, I only spend about a total of four or five hours each week clipping, filing, and mailing, and I do most of this while I am watching television or occupying myself in some way. Thus, I get myself into a habit and use my time effectively.

That covers the basics of the POP Blocks. Next, let's remember our "Supershopper boot camp." Do some research on your own during your next few trips through the supermarket. Take a look at how prices compare from brand to brand and from store to store. Examine the layout of each supermarket, keeping yourself mindful of ways in which the store is trying to trick you into buying more than you need to. Check every "bargain" display, especially those at the ends of aisles, then double-check with the prices in the other aisles to see if these are actual deals.

Feel free to take a pen and paper to the stores and write down the prices of your favorite items. When you get home, take the average of the prices on each item. This should tell you not only what a good price is on your favorite products, but also which stores offer the best overall deals. Keep in mind, no one store will have all the best prices on everything, which is why we'll have to look into other factors in choosing which store or stores we shop at. That brings us to . . .

Step 2 Review: Choose Your Store

There are various types of grocery stores available nowadays. Mom-and-pop shops, while less common, offer friendly service, but are often the most pricey and have the smallest selection. Co-ops, small chains like C-Town and specialty stores like Trader Joe's are a happy medium between the mom-and-pop shops and full-on supermarkets, as they offer a pretty good selection and affordable prices. Supermarkets like Acme, Albertsons, and A&P have the best selection for the price and offer the most savings opportunities while still being manageable. The giant supercenters like Wal-Mart and Target generally have the lowest overall prices but have a somewhat smaller selection. What's more, they can be too overwhelming for the weekly shopping trip, and they will be the most likely purveyors of those random impulse buys. The warehouse stores probably will give you enough exercise for the day because of their vastness, and their product variety is more limited, though they do offer good buys. Additionally, not all warehouse stores accept coupons, although BJ's is now accepting manufacturers' coupons as well as their own coupons and Costco has its own booklet, mailed to each member, with coupon savings.

So the way I look at it, your best bet is to pick two supermarkets in your area that offer the best overall prices and deals. If you run out of milk or need a quick item for a dinner recipe, that's when you should run over to your local co-op or mom-and-pop shop, since you can zoom in and out quickly without being tempted to buy anything else. If you need a new inflatable pool and a set of lawn chairs in *addition* to whatever other groceries you want, that's the time to check in with your nearest supercenter or warehouse.

How to pick the right supermarket? As I mentioned above, overall store prices are important. You won't find one specific store that will *always* offer you the best deals, which is why it is important not to give your undying loyalty to a particular chain. Look in the store flyers week by week and take note of which stores offer the most consistent deals on *your* products. Each store is appealing to a certain demographic, and there will be subtle differences. Even still, you might find that in one particular week when you need more fruits and veggies, Pathmark has the greatest savings, while next week when you need lots of chicken Food Emporium will be offering the lower prices on that product.

Other factors to consider are the time and money spent on transportation; proximity is both a convenience and a money-saving opportunity. I don't mean you need to sit with a calculator and figure out the cost of driving to one store versus another—we're not trying to "drive" ourselves crazy here! Just keep store location in mind when you are making your shopping choices. In addition, consider things like how crowded the store gets, how friendly and knowledgeable the staff is, and how comfortable you feel when you step inside. Trust your gut. It will make the shopping experience more enjoyable, and since this book is all about getting the most out of your shopping trips, we should make it as fun as possible!

Once you have narrowed the selection based on the above criteria, be sure to ask the store managers about their coupon policies. Let's review the ones you should be most concerned with:

— Doubling or tripling coupons, and up to what price

— Stacking (accepting store and manufacturer coupons on the same item)

— Store loyalty programs (Does the store have a loyalty card? If so, how much does it discount? And what other benefits are available, e.g., a free Thanksgiving turkey with a minimum purchase?)

— Acceptance of Internet coupons

Most supermarkets do double on some basis, and almost all allow you to combine offers nowadays. Don't pick up a store card for every store you've ever been to. Not only will it be a nightmare to keep track of them all, but also you will be tempted to bounce around to tons of different stores since you figure, "Well, I have the card. I may as well use it." The key is to keep focused on two or three stores at most, the stores that will consistently offer you the greatest savings.

Supermarket owners and managers are businesspeople. They are intent on getting you to spend your money so that *they* will profit. This is one reason why you shouldn't feel any loyalty to one store over another. They are all trying to do the same thing. It is vital, however, to recognize the most common gimmicks they employ to keep you coming back for more. Let's briefly go over the big ones, shall we?

— *Advertisements:* Stores will often advertise products in flyers, in magazines, or at the store itself to move them off the shelves. Just because a product is being offered at a "special low rate!" it is not necessarily a deal compared to the same product of a different brand.

— *New product promotions:* Manufacturers offer thousands of new products each year, and store managers know that the best way to sell these products is to make the "newness" of said items as exciting as possible. Trust me: in most cases, there is no difference between "Regular" flavor and "Original!" or "Classic!!" But if you do want to try a brand-new item, always look for the high-value coupon offered along with many new products.

— *Featured items or end-of-aisle displays:* Those huge pyramids with big signs offering massive savings at the end of the aisle? Don't be fooled. Sometimes these "bargains" are merely lures to sell products that are near their expiration date or have not been selling.

Store managers employ endless other tactics to get you to see the most expensive products and to buy things that are advertised as "sale prices" when in fact they are just the same, if not more pricey, than other brands. Don't forget: just because something is a lower price than its sister brand does *not* mean you're getting a better deal! We have to factor in the *next* step of the Supershopping system first: coupons!

Step 3 Review: Use Coupon Power

You can regularly save upwards of 50%–65%, as I do, by using step 3 of the system. With the right know-how and attitude, you will find that coupons are the biggest advantage shoppers have in combating rising prices at the store. Unfortunately, the vast majority of coupons are never redeemed, leaving literally billions of dollars in "free money" in the garbage. I think it's safe to say Americans are missing out on one of the most obvious and easy-to-use boons they have at their disposal when it comes to saving money.

> Unfortunately, the vast majority of coupons are never redeemed, leaving literally billions of dollars in "free money" in the garbage.

Coupons come in two varieties: manufacturers' coupons issued directly by the large corporations that make most of the products we buy and store (or in-ad) coupons, which are only good at a particular chain. Many stores allow "stacking"—that is, using *both* types of coupons on the same product—especially the larger chains. Some stores will now accept competitors' in-ad coupons to give you the best value. Far and away, most coupons out there are for nationally advertised brands, as these major manufacturers are the ones with the most money and can afford to spend billions each year on marketing costs.

This is why a major tenet of the Supershopping system is that we *must stick with national brands*. Store brands are, on the whole, cheaper at first glance, and most systems out there will tell you simply to buy the "cheapest" product. Supershoppers go one step further, however, and use coupons to lower the price of the national brand products and end up with a bill much lower than they would have if they were buying only store brands.

Always make sure to check the store flyers for the bargains your stores are offering that week. Once you have compared these prices to your shopping list generated earlier, match the sales with the coupons you already have to maximize savings.

Where do we get these coupons? Let us review the best places to look:

— *Sunday newspaper:* Still by far the best source for coupons on a consistent basis. If you don't get the newspaper, find someone who does and clip away!

— *Magazines:* If you aren't a magazine reader, don't buy subscriptions just for the coupons. Look in doctors' offices, salons, and so on, or ask your friends to give you their magazines once they are done with them.

— *Stores:* Many coupons are affixed directly to the packaging of the products. But the Supershopper *never* buys a product just for the coupon on the back! Blinking coupon dispensers are a great source, and they are located right in the store aisles. Additionally, special displays often have coupons attached. Being alert is your best asset in finding these.

—*The Internet:* Printable and digital coupons are starting to become more popular means of getting coupons. Check manufacturers' websites and Coupons.com (or just do a search for "printable coupons" and find your own favorite sites).

—*Home mailers:* Once you have begun saving with coupons, signing up for loyalty cards, and refunding through the mail, you will start to see an influx of "home mailers" delivered right to your doorstep or to your e-mail in-box. These will often clue you in to great deals you would otherwise never have known about.

—*Select Coupon Program (www.selectcouponprogram .com):* My own business program offers $25 worth of coupons each month and allows members to choose from over eight hundred different products, not to mention all the great printable coupon websites, blogs, and discussion board tips found on our site. This beats home mailers since you get to decide which cash-offs fit your shopping needs.

The point is that you should always be on the lookout for coupon offers. Get in the habit of clipping and printing coupons whenever you are skimming a magazine or surfing the Web, and before long, you will find that your coupon file is bigger than you ever expected!

Keep your coupons well organized so you don't waste time and energy searching all over the house for that much-needed cash-off. If you like my system of a coupon file, go with that. But whatever system you use, make sure it is one you can understand. Organize alphabetically by category and within each category by product name, (if you do it the same way as your shopping list it will be that much easier to remember what lives where). Keep the coupons with the closest expiration dates near the front, and remember to check your file frequently to avoid walking into the store with a handful of expired cash-offs.

> **Keep your coupons well organized so you don't waste time and energy searching all over the house for that much-needed cash-off.**

There is absolutely no reason to feel embarrassed about going into the store with a ton of cash-offs; the store and the manufacturers *want* you to use them. It tells them that consumers are buying their products again and again, and it helps them gauge which products sell the best. Furthermore, the manufacturers not only reimburse the stores for the cost of the coupon itself, but they also pay them an additional "handling fee." If you feel shy about using coupons, as many Americans do, remember that you are doing both the store and the manufacturers a service by using their offers.

Just try to keep your time at the checkout brief and well planned. Don't just dump a pile of cash-offs on top of your products—have them organized and in a neat pile ready to hand to the cashier as soon as he or she begins tallying your total. This is a courtesy to both the cashier and the customers waiting in line behind you.

And speaking of walking through the checkout aisle . . . let's take a look at step 4 of the Supershopping system, where we actually walk through the aisles together!

Step 4 Review: Shop Smart

The main components of this step involve understanding the layout and dynamic of the supermarket itself. We've already covered many of the psychological marketing ploys manufacturers and store managers use to get you to buy products on impulse, but now let's look at how this plays out in the aisles.

Pricing plays a huge part in our mental blockage against major savings. First off, $4.99 *does not equal* "four dollars and some change." With tax, it's over $5. This is obvious when you think about it, but many people are inclined to round down for some odd reason. Our brains process the first number (the "4") and assume that is the most important number. Supermarkets know this and use it to their full advantage. Always throw in a few dollars for tax when you are looking at your shopping cart.

Product placement and store layout is a true science to store owners, and the Supershopper is aware of the mind games being played and fights them every step of the way. Rather than revisiting each ploy in detail as we did in chapter 4, here's just a quick recap to jog your memory:

— *Visit only necessary aisles:* There is no need to walk through every aisle in the store. Scan ahead, and before you walk in the aisles, first look at all the "top-of-aisle" signs (the ones that list the product categories) and make a game plan for yourself.

— *Cover the schnoz:* Your nose is your worst enemy in the grocery store. Smell is linked to appetite and the store will entice you with every delicious aroma it can. Fresh-baked breads and sliced meats are always in the back, forcing you to walk through the entire store to see what smells so good. Never enter a store hungry.

—*Ignore displays of related products:* Special displays of some products will often be placed near related items even when they don't fit in with the top-of-aisle sign. I'm not talking about different brands of the same product, but rather products that logically "go together," like pasta and pasta sauce, pancake mix and syrup, soda and chips, etc. You will find that most of the specially placed items' counterparts are available for less in the aisles in which they belong. Thus, don't buy your tomato sauce when you're in the pasta aisle. Go to the section specifically for sauces.

—*Shop the perimeter:* The middle aisles have the least useful items, and the back and sides of the store will feature the most top-list items. For example, when in the dairy aisle hunting for milk and eggs, you will undoubtedly have to walk past the puddings, whipped cream, and other nonessentials to get there. My best advice is to follow your list and keep your eyes on the prize.

—*Look beyond eye level:* The Supershopper never looks only at the eye-level products, as he or she knows that these are the items the store knows will be the most tempting (and often the most pricey). Look above and below for the best deals.

—*Beware of shuffling:* Shuffling, where the store manager will rearrange products as if on whim, is a way to get you to check out new or poorly selling items. Since you are used to your store's layout, you will head to where your products usually sit, only to find some other item is now on that shelf. It's unavoidable, so don't let their head tricks get to you. Politely ask the staff where your item was moved to.

And these are only a handful of the tips we should keep in mind when walking down the aisle. As always, the name of the game is awareness. Be a savvy shopper and you will be a Supershopper.

Store loyalty (or rewards) programs have come a long way in the past decade, and while many store owners see them as not economically viable and more trouble than they're worth, they can still be a great tool for the Supershopper. Loyalty programs are different from loyalty cards in that they involve you bringing something *back* to the store or doing something additional after your shopping trip to receive the rewards. The example I mentioned in chapter 4 was the printer and printer cartridge recycling program at Staples, but there are dozens of others. Look online at the websites for stores you visit and see what programs they have that you might be missing out on.

Also, it doesn't hurt to sign up for the loyalty cards at the stores you frequent, but first, ask what the policies are and what kind of discount you are getting. If the cashier doesn't know, ask the store manager for details.

I can understand that many of us are hesitant to give up our information to massive chains, and this is not a wholly unfounded fear. The systems are not yet 100% secure, and signing up for one store's program may run the risk of getting you on mailing lists for other big chains (this is what the industry calls "information sharing")—so if you don't want to deal with spam, either bypass this step or give an alternate e-mail address created specifically to receive store offers.

Loyalty programs and cards can be wonderful ways to save off your final bill, and they are available at drugstores, hardware stores, pet supply stores, and chain supermarkets. You can leave the cards at home, as the store can bring up your account using your telephone number or zip code in most cases.

Now that we've discussed the best way to make it to the checkout with our groceries, let us not forget our simple rules when we arrive at the register to make life easier for us, the cashier, and those in line behind us. Have your coupons ready, keep your products organized on the conveyer belt, remind the cashier in advance that you will be using coupons, don't bother double-bagging except with heavy products or bring your own reusable bags, and keep a sharp eye on the total as your items are scanned to catch any potential errors. All of these pieces of advice are just common sense.

It's time to head out of the store and take another quick look at the final aspect of the Supershopping system—refunds!

Step 5 Review: Aggressive Saving

Refunding, for many Supershoppers, is that extra mile we go to generate a steady, tax-free income with very little effort. As with the rest of my program, refunding is easy once you get into the habit of doing it, and you can easily make a few thousand dollars a year alone with refunds.

All you have to do is locate the refund forms in the various places they appear: the stores themselves, newspapers and magazines, straight from the manufacturers, on the Internet, and from other refunders like yourself. Trading brings us Supershoppers together and ensures big winnings for everyone. By providing access to each other's resources (like qualifiers, cash-offs, and rebate forms), we can maximize our profits by gaining what we cannot acquire on our own. Trading is a great way to simultaneously get rid of unneeded qualifiers or cash-offs and receive missing ones in return.

Refunding newsletters like my *Refundle Bundle* are a great source for finding people who need certain forms and for identifying the refunds from your favorite manufacturers. This community aspect is what makes me love Supershopping so much. A great example of this team playing mentality popped up just recently when a subscriber to *Refundle Bundle* passed along a great tip: do "round-robin" shopping with your extended family by sending coupons and a short note to various family members and asking them to respond—this creates a sort of ongoing "family reunion" via coupons!

Once you know the offers and have the forms, file them away while you collect the necessary qualifiers. This brings us into our Refunder's S.O.S.:

— *Save everything:* Qualifiers come in many shapes and sizes, and it is crucial that you keep as many packaging wrappers, labels, and hang tabs as is humanly possible. You never know what the manufacturer will ask for!

— *Organize your forms and qualifiers:* It is impossible to keep track of all of these forms and qualifiers if you don't keep them well organized. My shoe box method works for me, so just find a system that makes sense to you. Condense the wrappers and flatten out labels so everything fits in a small, compact space.

— *Send away for your refunds:* Squirreling away all these forms and qualifiers won't pay off until you send in your completed forms with the appropriate qualifiers to the address on the form. Make personal address labels to cut down on time. Do the mailings while occupying yourself otherwise: watching TV, talking on the phone, waiting for water to boil, whatever floats your refunding boat. And don't forget about the Internet: many manufacturers have implemented online refund submissions. RiteAid. com is one of the best online submission retailers. Monthly it offers upwards of $500 in offers. You enter information from your cash register receipts and the site keeps track of your rebates. At the end of the month, simply hit the "submit" button, and your refund is mailed to your home. Staples is using this same concept. All their rebates can be either submitted online or by mail. A great time saver, and all your information is already stored through your shopper card.

The Refunder's S.O.S. is a simple guide to getting cash back or free coupons for products you have bought, and it's all tax-free!

Refunding has a much higher net potential than does couponing, since most cash-offs are for no more than $1 or $2, while refunds can earn you as much as $5 for a single offer, or a free product coupon for something you might need later on. Still, very few people actively refund, and it's understandable since refunds aren't quite as in-your-face as coupons are in our day-to-day lives. But as a Supershopper, we know the value of staying aware of potential saving opportunities, and we won't let these thousands of dollars go to waste like the Normal Shopper will!

Just don't get discouraged if you don't see enormous savings right away. It takes time to build enough qualifiers and forms to start making the big bucks back, and even once you have sent away for the forms, it can take several weeks to receive checks. Be patient, and don't write angry letters to the companies demanding your money. If it has taken more than six or eight weeks, a short note, a call to the toll-free number or e-mail explaining the situation, with the date you sent your form in, isn't a bad idea.

Do anything you can to avoid a rejection letter: check the expiration dates on all forms, make sure you are sending in the correct qualifiers (you have to be exact!), and fill out all the forms completely and accurately. This will help guarantee that your check will come promptly.

That does it for refunds, but what about those free gifts we talked about? Premiums are a fun way to stack up on cute gifts for the holidays or add items to your casual-wear wardrobe, like hats and T-shirts. The principle with premiums is exactly the same as with refunds: send in qualifiers with the form and receive a free gift in the mail. The only cost with most premiums is shipping, as with refunds, so only send in for as many premiums as you feel is worth it.

Some premiums, furthermore, are "cash-plus" deals, meaning you have to send in not only the necessary qualifiers and forms, but also a small fee. This will obviously come out to much less than the gift itself would, and the cash-plus premiums are always the nicest products. Still, do this at your own discretion and try to remember that *saving money* is the reason we became Supershoppers. Free gifts are a great bonus, but don't get so wrapped up in premiums that you forget what the Supershopping system is about.

And that's all there is! Five easy steps to saving thousands of dollars a year on your groceries.

WHERE DO YOU FIT IN?

We've talked a lot about shopping, saving, and spending, but it's sometimes hard to find how *you* are connected to all this. Well, the good news is that more and more people in every age range have switched to coupons, and the trend is on the rise. College student needing some help on groceries? New parents trying to feed extra mouths? Retirees with a small pension looking to ease the burden of inflation? Everyone can be a Supershopper, and everyone *should* be a Supershopper. There is no reason to think that just because of your age or location you cannot save big at the grocery store.

Geographic Demographics

As you may have figured, the major U.S. cities are the leading areas for coupon-using households (households using coupons once a week or more). The top two are Milwaukee, Wisconsin, with 40%, and Rochester, New York, with 38%. My home city, New York, is not far behind with 33%. Other notably high-ranking coupon cities include Pittsburgh; Columbus; Syracuse; Baltimore; Indianapolis; Tampa; Knoxville; Chicago; Detroit; San Antonio; Washington, DC; Portland; Phoenix; Los Angeles; Las Vegas; and Honolulu, all with over one-quarter of the population using coupons on a weekly basis or more. The national average is around 27% (all info courtesy of Scarborough Research). Not bad, America! But we could be doing better.

As you can see, it doesn't matter what part of the country you are from; coupons are readily available all over the United States, and while major cities of course have the highest redemption rates, there are still plenty of coupons to be had in smaller rural or suburban communities (just look at me—I'm from Westchester County and I don't have a problem!).

People who subscribe to the Sunday newspaper are 15% more likely to use coupons, which is no surprise since the Sunday paper accounts for more than a third of the total coupons out there. And no matter where you live, there is a Sunday newspaper available to you, not to mention national magazines and in-store circulars.

Age Demographics

The traditional belief that couponing is "for the older folks" is quickly being broken down as more and more youths are discovering a need to save money in these trying times and realizing that this means of cutting back on expenses is a fully valid system.

According to Scarborough, the largest bracket of coupon users in the United States is young to middle-aged parents supporting several children. The next category is people over fifty-four years old, and people below age thirty-five are the smallest category. However, these numbers are almost completely reversed in terms of the growth of coupon use. For example, those same people in the under–thirty-five age group have had by far the largest increase in coupon use recently, with 57% reporting using more coupons than ever before. The fifty-four–plus crowd, on the other hand, has only had an increase of roughly 25%, and the middle group is somewhere in between.

What does this mean? It means that no one is *stopping* using coupons. It's clear that once people begin saving money with couponing, they are more than likely going to continue doing so. In fact, more people from the younger age bracket than ever before are using coupons. One reason is that coupons have become a more acceptable societal norm, and people under thirty-five have reported being much less self-conscious when it comes to using cash-offs in the supermarket. This kind of news brings a smile to my face: there is no reason to be self-conscious about saving money!

Socioeconomic Demographics

As we've established, people all across the country are using coupons, and they fall into all income brackets. However, there are a higher percentage of coupon users in higher-income households, which is odd to me since you would think that those in dire economic straits would jump at the chance to save money on their escalating bills.

I believe that the principal cause for the lack of coupon use is simply a lack of knowledge of the means of acquiring and using cash-offs. One of my purposes in writing this book is to enlighten everyone out there (regardless of his or her background) as to the benefits of couponing and refunding. Hopefully with this book as a guide, more people than ever will realize the advantages of the Supershopping system.

Now that you have a sense of where you fit into the bigger picture of savings, perhaps you can identify which areas of Supershopping fit best for you. Regardless, you now have all the tools you need to become a true Supershopper, and that means my work is done. Your work, however, is just beginning. Thank you for joining me on this journey, and I hope my system will prove to be as useful for you and your family as it has been for the millions who have joined the Supershopping family over the past three decades.

The final pages of this book are just additional little tidbits I thought you might enjoy reading. First, I'll answer some FAQs and list some important terms. Finally, you can read testimonials of other "satisfied customers."

Happy shopping!

APPENDIX 1

Frequently Asked Questions

···

AN EXCLUSIVE Q&A WITH THE COUPON QUEEN

I've been interviewed on radio and television programs from New York to California, and I've had to field hundreds of questions about my system.

No doubt many of these same questions occurred to you as you read the foregoing chapters. Although I hope I've answered some of them for you already, clarifying the less obvious aspects of Supershopping would probably be helpful at this point for even the most attentive reader. In addition, there are some issues I haven't touched on, which I'd like to clear up now.

The advantages of Supershopping seem almost self-evident to me, but I've been an active refunder and coupon clipper for almost forty years now, and I realize that people with less savings experience than I may be curious about elements of the system I haven't yet explained. To them—and to all of you who still have misgivings about Supershopping—I offer this Q&A.

Q. *Why should I listen to you over the dozens of others who claim to be the "foremost experts" in the field?*

A. No one has ever directly asked me this question, but I'm sure it is floating around in some people's minds, and it is a very fair question. The fact is, much of the advice I give is the same or at least similar to the advice given by the other leading shopping experts. We do differ somewhat in the strategies we use to reach the goal of saving money. For instance, I believe my system is unique in suggesting purchasing national brand products since these products offer the best sales and discounts. Other programs advise you to focus on store brands, which I believe to be not only more expensive in the long run, but also of a slightly lower quality than the national brands. I know for a fact that I also promote refunding and rebating more than almost any other money-saving program. But what we all have in common is that we want to help you save money. Some people prefer my system; others do not. Most shoppers, however, create their own personalized version of Supershopping, incorporating knowledge from a variety of sources and doing what fits best with their lifestyle.

I will say this, however. I have been couponing and refunding for nearly four decades and have been around long enough to see the cyclical pattern of the economy and the food market; I have taken what I know and improved my system into something I can call close to perfect. I have tried literally every system out there, checked out every major supermarket in the nation, gone to nearly every major couponing website, and dealt with every single major food manufacturer in the United States, and purely from a numbers standpoint, no other system is as time-considerate and cost-effective as Supershopping. This is not bragging; it is simply the objective truth.

This is not to say, of course, that you should discount the information and advice given by other coupon experts. Some are much more linked in with the technological aspects of saving and may know some things I do not. But the fact of the matter is, 99% of the couponing systems out there, which sprouted up mostly during the recession in the late 1980s or just recently with the economic downturn, are in some way birthed from Supershopping, which has been around since 1973 and has had time to learn and grow. They say imitation is the best form of flattery and I think this is also a testament to how well Supershopping really works: as I travel the country, there are so many local coupon princesses that prove this system works.

Q. *Fine, you're amazing, I believe you. But you're practically a professional shopper! What about the rest of us? I clip coupons regularly but the whole idea of sending in forms and qualifiers for refunds seems out of my scope. How much can I reasonably expect to save?*

A. You're right that I've become almost an expert shopper. I do devote a good deal of time to my system, and I don't deny that it's my experience and large file of cash-offs and qualifiers that let me save thousands each year. But even the novice Supershopper can realize very good savings, and with a little effort *anyone* can easily save 25% off their bill and also make back a solid 10% by sending in qualifiers. If you spend the national average of

$114 per week on groceries, that's a savings of $28 per week with coupons and $11 per week back on refunds, or $2,028 per year that you wouldn't have had otherwise. That's the bare minimum. With a modest effort, that number will climb even higher, amounting to as much as 65%–80% of your yearly groceries spending, or an average of $4,368.

The amount of money you save by using my system depends to a great extent on how rigorously you apply the principles of Supershopping to your own personal shopping habits. If you become alert to sales, clip coupons faithfully, and get involved with refunding through the newsletter network, I see no reason why, within a few months, you can't be saving just as much on your bills as I am: that is, about 50%–65% every week.

Q. *I've been shopping at some of the dollar stores in my neighborhood. I've picked up some very good buys for $1. I still use coupons when items are on sale in the supermarket, but these savings were too good to pass up. What's your opinion?*

A. Dollar stores are a great source of discount buys, especially for nonfood items. I, too, pick up some good deals on aluminum goods (foil wrap and disposable aluminum trays) and paper products (especially gift bags, cards, and paper plates and cups). For food products you have to check the expiration dates very carefully. If no date is printed on it, pass up the product and stick to the supermarket.

In addition, these dollar stores offer items manufactured overseas that may not be under strict regulations, so toys can have high lead content. And not long ago there was an issue that toothpaste coming from other countries did not follow our FDA rules. Lastly, like store brands or generic brands, some of the paper goods or plastic garbage bags are inferior quality, and are you really saving money if the bags keep ripping and you have to use two bags?

Q. *This is more of a suggestion than a question. I have a lot of extra coupons, some I trade, but others I use to buy products when I see them on sale. I had four 75¢ coupons on Colgate toothpaste, which my store doubled to $1.50. With Colgate on sale for $1.99, I bought four tubes. I used these and other great toiletry deals to donate to my local food pantry. They were a big hit.*

A.   I hope others will take your suggestion and use coupons to save for local donations. What a great idea to help our neighbors and friends. Don't forget the local pet shelters, too. They love donations of extra pet food supplies.

Q. *I often find coupons that don't specify a size or type of product. I notice this particularly in the Health and Beauty Aid category. Also, my store boasts tons of trial-size products. Can I use my coupons on trial-size goods and on goods of any size?*

A.   You can use your coupon on any size package as long as there are no specifics as to size or quantity. This, of course, includes the trial-size goods you mentioned! As a matter of fact a $1 coupon against a trial size will often get you the product free.

Q. *Yikes! I work nine to five and so does my spouse! It sounds as if you live, eat, and breathe Supershopping. Just how much time do you spend every week on the various parts of your system? Should I expect to commit my every waking hour to this system in order to become a Supershopper?*

A. It's a common misconception that Supershoppers spend their days clipping coupons and their nights dreaming about labels. I am a wife and the mother of four grown children, and if attending to my system took that much time I couldn't have stuck with it for a week while my boys were growing up. I'd never have gotten anything else done.

I spend about four or five hours a week cutting coupons and filling out forms, removing and sorting qualifiers, filing, and sending away for offers. That's a little less than an hour a day, and I try to make it seem like even less by doing most of my coupon and refund work while I'm also doing something else, such as riding in the car or watching TV. A less organized shopper may end up spending a little more time, a more organized one a little less.

I know several people who spend more time than this each week on a hobby. And there are very few hobbies that regularly cut your grocery bill in half.

Q. *Other shopping systems say exactly the opposite of you in regard to buying store brands vs. national brands. Isn't it easier just to forget about the whole couponing business and shop for the cheaper store brands?*

A. Perhaps it would be *easier*, but you have to ask yourself: are you doing this as a convenience, or do you want to become a Supershopper to save as much money as possible and ease the burden of rising prices? It's true: store brands *do* have a cheaper face value; there's no denying that. But the trouble with buying them is that they are produced by smaller, independent manufacturers who simply cannot compete with the major firms in terms of shopping incentives such as sales, coupons, and refunds.

Store brands generally are priced 15% cheaper than the nationals, but active couponing can cut your bill by 25% or 30% *easily*—and this isn't even counting the possibility of a future refund on that Kellogg's box that you will never get on the store brand. Simple arithmetic will show you that Supershopping for the nationals can easily save you 10%–15% right off the top over Normal Shopping for the "bargain" line. If you achieve the 65% savings that many of my readers have, we're talking an additional *50% less* on overall price than the store brand! How is there any question?

If you don't practice refunding and couponing, of course, the store brands *are* cheaper than the nationals. But now you're talking about paying 85¢ for a store brand versus $1 for the known brand name. What Supershopping offers you is the opportunity to buy the item that usually costs $1 for as little as 50¢.

Q. *Okay, so you swear by national brand names. Which ones, in terms of your savings system, are the ones I should especially watch out for?*

A. As a rule, coupons and refunds come not from individual products, but from the several giant firms that manufacture most of our processed food and goods. Therefore, what you really have to look for is not so much the trademark name but the big company that produced it and stands behind it. For example, you'll never get any money back from Jell-O per se. The people who will send you your Jell-O refund or issue coupons are at Kraft Foods, the conglomerate that produces everything from Jell-O to Maxwell House coffee to Minute Rice to Log Cabin syrup. Therefore, when you're focusing on coupons and refunds, look for the name of the manufacturer; it will be printed on the package somewhere.

Here are some of the most savings-awarding big-name manufacturers and subsidiaries:

Betty Crocker	Hershey's
Borden	Kellogg
Campbell	Kraft Foods
French's	Pillsbury
Philip Morris	Procter & Gamble
General Mills	Keebler
Green Giant	Unilever

On the refunding end, some of the best companies are Kraft Foods and General Mills. I've also had very good experiences with these companies and brands: Nestlé, Nabisco, Ragú, Kellogg, Libby's, Colgate-Palmolive, S.C. Johnson, Johnson & Johnson, Dove, and Borden.

This is not to suggest that other companies do not offer coupons and refunds. Just keep your eyes open for coupons and refund offers in newspapers and magazines, in stores, and on the products themselves. And do check out the websites of your favorite brands. Many have coupons you can print out or sign up for. Manufacturers want you to buy their products, and offering savings opportunities is one of the most effective marketing tools they have.

Q. *Do you find more offers at certain times of the year than at others?*

A. You don't really find more of them, but you find different kinds, since some offers are synchronized with seasonal shopping patterns. I've noticed a lot of savings on ham around Easter time, candy around Halloween, and turkey at Thanksgiving. In the summer, various beverage manufacturers always offer free gifts (premiums) for use in the garden; we've gotten gloves, a barbecue set, and tools. At Christmas many of the big toy companies offer both refunds and coupons. And batteries coupons and rebates are big for all those toys.

Q. *Are there refunds and coupons on all kinds of products, or only new and exotic ones?*

A. There are refunds and coupons on *everything*. From time to time they repeat themselves, so the smart Supershopper knows that getting $1 back this week on Del Monte tomatoes doesn't mean she should throw out all her Del Monte labels or coupons; they're sure to come in handy again. Every major manufacturer of food or household products offers savings on a regular basis, and the order is generally cyclical. That is why I insist that you must be flexible and willing to switch stores and brands, while other coupon experts will advise you to stick to one store. After all, if you just missed a big sale on milk at "your one and only store," do you really want to wait two or three weeks for that sale to hit again? Of course not! You will most likely find said sale at another store the following week.

Refunds and cash-offs are most frequently offered on paper goods, household products such as cleansers and detergents, and all kinds of processed foods: that is, items that have been boxed, frozen, or canned. You can't find very many offers for money back on unprocessed foods such as meat and produce, although there are occasional exceptions.

Q. *Since you always shop with refunds in mind, don't you often find yourself buying things you don't need, just to get the refund?*

A. I never buy a product I can't use just to get the refund. That would defeat the whole purpose of the system, which is to save money. Sometimes, however, I will go in for a "bulk buy," but only in the case of staple items or products that won't go bad sitting on the shelf. I will (and have) bought several cans of tomato sauce to cash in quickly on a refund that demands, say, five UPCs; but I would never stock up on something like bread—or any perishable—because it would just end up going to waste.

The essence of Supershopping is using the supermarkets' offers to shop more sensibly than you do now. I have a whole shelf full of label-less cans whose labels have gone to make me money. (I know what they are because I mark them with a Magic Marker.) I would not buy one item that I could not use. That would merely be wasting space. Not to mention money.

Q. *With all that mailing you do on refunds, how much do you spend on postage?*

A. Postage costs are inevitable in refunding, and they're difficult to reduce beyond a certain minimum. Since I send out about one hundred requests each month, the cost of those first-class stamps is inevitable. Envelopes (of course I buy the cheapest available, in bulk) come to perhaps $2 a month. Staples has 500 of the #10 envelope for $8.29. I look at this expense as a kind of service fee to myself, and I take the cash for it directly out of my refunding money, so I won't feel the bite somewhere else. Considering that I'm getting back some $200–$250 per month from the companies, I don't think it's an excessive expense. Another thing to note is that I keep the cash I get back in an interest-bearing account. That interest helps defray postage costs.

There are ways to reduce costs even further. In any company correspondence where you can use a postcard instead of a letter, you should do so. That goes for correspondence with fellow newsletter readers, too. In newsletter exchanges, you should favor advertisers who include "EPOP"—"each pay own postage"—in their ads: that will let you split the postage costs with another refunder.

Q. *I've heard of schools having "labels (or box tops) for education" programs. I have two children in school, and I would like more information on how to help their school.*

A. There are two excellent programs that use the concept— school communities collect labels and box tops from certain product brands and redeem them for cash or merchandise for the school. In each case the number of labels accumulated determines the rewards. In the case of General Mills (www.boxtops4education.com), your school earns 10¢ for each label submitted. A great way to purchase needed items. Campbell's program (www.labelsforeducation.com) offers equipment and materials for art, academics, and athletics. The concept is the same: the more labels submitted the better.

Q. ***What do the companies think of your super savings?***

A. In general, they don't mind at all. They issue coupons and refund offers, after all, as a kind of "reward" for buying their products—and Supershoppers are not known as skimpers in that regard. In general, I've found the companies to be consistently helpful and in accord with what I'm doing.

Q. ***What advice can you give to those of us who are just getting started in Supershopping? What's the best way for us to realize the benefits of the system in the shortest possible time?***

A. Probably the first thing you should do is to subscribe to a refunding newsletter like RefundleBundle.com, it will put you in contact with other shoppers in a similar position and enable you to profit from the contacts and experience of the entire refunding community. Beyond that, the best advice I can give you is to open your eyes when you shop, to catch those sales and offers, to use coupons, and to follow the Refunder's S.O.S. outlined in chapter 5: *save* everything, *organize* your savings system, and *send* away regularly for your refunds.

There's no mystery about Supershopping. For me it's been the result of realizing that I'd save more by shopping intelligently rather than blindly and taking advantage of the many manufacturers' offers that are available to anyone who has ever pushed a cart down a supermarket aisle. You can take advantage of them as easily as I have. All you have to do is to know that they are there, and then put in a modest amount of effort to ensure that you get your slice of the Supershopping pie.

This book, I trust, will have given you a foundation on which to build your own Supershopping style. Perhaps, by adopting its precepts, you will come up with a system of cashing in that realizes even greater savings than my own. If so, I'd love to hear from you about it. One of the real joys of being a regular refunder is being able to exchange advice and ideas with shoppers all around the country. I hope, therefore, that you'll take this book not as a bible, but as a guide: in other words, something that can help you bring out your own individual savings talents every time you go to the store.

In a sense, this book is an attempt to open the lines of communication between the hard-core couponers and refunders who are now saving so much on their bills and the vast untapped community of shoppers who want to save but don't know how.

If you're one of that community, don't be shy. Drop me a line. Together, we can all cash in.

APPENDIX 2

Glossary

· ·

THE REFUNDER'S DICTIONARY

This glossary of abbreviations and terms is a compendium of those I use throughout this book as well as some you will come across in other couponing and refunding resources.

BOGOF. Buy one, get one free. Using a cash-off coupon along with a BOGOF deal can net you incredible savings. Also known as "BOGO."

bundling. The common marketing practice of grouping items together for one price in the hopes of selling more. Oftentimes these are not real bargains (the prices are not lower), but rather items the store wants to get rid of. Also called "multiple-unit pricing."

cash-off. A certificate good for a reduction in the purchase price of a specified product. Cash-offs are redeemed at the grocery store. Also called "cents-off."

cash-plus. An offer that requires that cash, in addition to qualifiers, accompany the request. Also called "money-plus."

catalina. A coupon printed along with or on the back of a cash register tape. Often catalinas are linked to the products you just bought or have bought in the past from that same store.

CB. Cardboard backing. The backing behind a pad of store forms, which generally gives an address to write to for a form, or for the refund itself, if all the forms are gone.

C/D. Complete deal, or complete cash deal. An exchange in which two refunders trade "packages" of all the material needed to cash in on a given refund: that is, forms plus proofs of purchase.

C/O. See "cash-off."

CPG. Consumer packaged goods. Consumable goods like food, beverages, and cleaning products, as opposed to long-lasting items such as cars and furniture.

CPI. Consumer price index. A measure used to estimate the average price of goods purchased by households in any given region (or on a national level).

CPN. Coupon. A cash-off generally available on packages and in magazines, newspapers, and home mailers.

CRT. Cash register tape. Manufacturers occasionally ask

for these as proofs of purchase in addition to the regular qualifiers.

DM. Direct mailer. See "HM."

doubling. A practice by which the store gives you *twice* the value of your coupons instead of the face value. Thus, a 50¢ coupon is actually worth $1, and a $1 coupon is worth $2. Each store sets its own limits.

ED. Expiration date usually found on a coupon or refund offer.

EPOP. Each pay own postage. This indicates that each partner in an exchange is responsible for his or her own mailing costs.

form. An order blank that must accompany the required qualifiers in certain cash refund offers. Forms are found in stores, magazines, newspapers, and home mailers.

Grocery iQ. A grocery list software application, owned by Coupons, Inc., that lets you create and edit your list on your iPhone or Android phone.

H/F. Handling fee. A nominal charge—usually 25¢, sometimes 50¢—some newsletter advertisers require as reimbursement for sending out forms or qualifiers. Sometimes called a "shuffling fee."

HM. Home mailer. A flyer or brochure sent to residences by manufacturers eager to interest potential customers in their products. A home mailer may contain a coupon, free sample, or refund form. Also called a "direct mailer" (DM).

HT. Hang tag. A type of store form or coupon that is found hung around the neck of a bottle or jar.

in-ad coupons. Coupons valid only at a particular store. Recently, however, some supermarkets have begun accepting in-ad coupons from their competitors.

LSASE. Long self-addressed stamped envelope. See "SASE."

LTD. Limited offer. Indicates that the offer advertised is restricted to a particular area of the country.

MF. Magazine form. A refund offer form found in a magazine.

money-plus. See "cash-plus."

national brand. Products made by a large manufacturer like Kellogg, Procter & Gamble, Kraft, or Campbell. Also called "brand name" (sometimes "name brand").

NED. No expiration date. Indicates that the offer or coupon advertised has no prearranged closing date, and may therefore expire at any time.

NF. Newspaper form. A refund order form found in a newspaper.

POP. Proof of purchase. In one sense, this refers to the proof of purchase seals found on many products. It also means any qualifier, but the first meaning generally applies in newsletter listings.

POP Blocks. The three building blocks of Supershopping: *Plan* ahead. *Organize* yourself. *Practice, practice, practice!*

PP. Purchase price.

premium. Like a refund offer, a premium is a small gift acquired either for free or for a highly discounted price upon sending in a form and qualifiers.

qualifier. Any part of a package that a manufacturer demands as a proof of purchase to accompany the request for a refund. Common qualifiers include box tops, labels, cash register tapes, and POP and UPC seals.

rain check. The certificate a store gives you when it is out of an advertised special, so you can buy at the advertised price when the item is back in stock.

refund. A tax-free cash-back system whereby the consumer sends in to the manufacturer a simple form and a set of qualifiers (proof that a certain number of a particular product was purchased) and receives a check for money back. Also called a "rebate."

REQ. Required, as in "required form."

round-robin. A trading system in which several refunders from different locations cooperate to exchange forms, labels, and coupons. Each member of the group takes whatever he or she needs from the circulating material, replaces it with equivalent items, and mails it on around the circle.

SASE. Self-addressed stamped envelope. Many newsletter ads for trading and selling request these to help defray mailing expenses. Some ads specify a long envelope, designated "LSASE."

SF. Store form. A refund order form found in a store.

shelf shuffling. A common practice employed by most supermarket chains whereby the store manager regularly moves items to new locations in the store so shoppers have to walk around longer to find what they are looking for and hopefully make more purchases along the way.

SMP. Specially marked package. A package that the manufacturer has indicated contains either a coupon or a form for a refund offer.

store brand. Products manufactured and sold by a store or chain of stores. These are typically cheaper in base price but are rarely on sale and cannot be purchased with coupons (except in some special cases).

tripling. A practice by which the store will give you *thrice* the value of your coupons instead of the face value. Thus, a 50¢ coupon is actually worth a $1.50, and a $1 coupon is worth $3. This is much less common than doubling.

UPC. Universal Product Code. A series of lines over a code number that appears on nearly all supermarket items. The UPC speeds inventory-taking and facilitates computerization at the checkout. Often used as a proof of purchase.

1-4-1. An exchange in which the traders swap forms or qualifiers on an equal basis, one item returned for each one given.

APPENDIX 3

Testimonials

....

WHAT ARE OTHER SUPERSHOPPERS SAYING?

Over the years I have received many kind words from couponers, both novice and veteran. It always brings a smile to my face whenever I hear how my advice and help are allowing others to save enough to buy the things they really want in life.

"I've learned so much over the years and you helped quite a bit in the learning process. It isn't a challenge to me anymore. It is enjoyable. I love couponing. It may seem to be a lot of work, but the payoff is very good."
~LILLY P., BENTLEYVILLE, PA

❖

"I recently went shopping armed with all my coupons and I saved over $56. I went home happy. And my checkbook is happy, too."

~Marla B., Huntington Beach, CA

❖

"I have been refunding since I was in high school—almost 40 years! I am also the Freebie Queen, having obtained a free TV, hair dryer, toaster oven, several T-shirts, and numerous other items. Your 1979 book, Cashing In at the Checkout, has been my guide to my success in savings."

~Linda E., Beaumont, TX

❖

"With all of the store discounts, coupons, and cash back offers, I calculated a savings of approximately $90 on my last trip. I call that a successful weekend. It took a fair amount of work on my part to lay out where we bought what, but for the $90 in savings, it was well worth it. Thanks again!"

~Tom C., Royersford, PA

❖

"Susan Samtur is the smartest person I know. I save at least 60% every time I go shopping and I get approximately $50 a month in refunds. I met her on one of her shopping trips when she came to Chicago and I am so

glad I met her. She really is and always will be the 'Coupon Queen.'"

~BEN S., CHICAGO, IL

❖

"I just took two wonderful trips to Arizona, and believe me, with fares the way they are, it's nice to have my refund account for travel money. Long live the Coupon Queen!"

~ALICE D., EUGENE, OR

❖

"While exploring the internet, I found some of your videos on couponing and refunding, and I am amazed! I never thought I could generate the types of savings that I have! I regularly save 50% or more on my grocery bills now!

Refunding amazes me too! I currently have $50 coming back to me in rebates and refunds, as well as books of coupons and coupons for free stuff! I love it!

Thank you so much for all that you do with Refundle Bundle and being the Coupon Queen! It's all thanks to you!"

~CHARLES S, ISLE LA MOTTE, VT

❖

"Living in a rural area, you can still save money couponing. You just have to get more creative in your

use of coupons! One grocery store near me doubles coupons. I make good savings through coupon usage and mail-in rebates. Some of the items I buy using coupons are donated to my church's food pantry program. Coupons have many advantages.

~Virginia Ann S., Cobbs Creek, VA

❖